The Classes
They Remember

Learn how to use role-plays to bring history and literature to life! When students take on the roles of historical or literary figures, they develop a greater understanding of characters' identities and motivations, and are able to explore and reflect more deeply upon key issues and themes. In this new book from award-winning teacher David Sherrin, you'll find out how this lively instructional format will make teaching a more immersive, interactive, and memorable experience for your middle school and high school students. The book includes:

- a clear how-to guide to get the most out of role-playing in your class;
- ready-made units and lessons to get you started right away, complete with sample scripts, scaffolding worksheets, and assessment rubrics;
- templates and step-by-step instructions to help you design your own role-plays.

The pre-made units, which Sherrin spent years refining in his classroom, cover historical topics such as the rise of Nazi Germany and the Spanish conquest of the Aztecs. You'll also find fun and interactive role-plays based on literary works like *The Pearl* and *Fences*. These lessons will help students at all ability levels to become better communicators, problem-solvers, and creative thinkers.

David Sherrin an English and Social Studies teacher at Harvest Collegiate High School in New York City, where he is also the Social Studies Department Chair and the Master Teacher. At the 2014 NCSS Annual Conference, he was the recipient of the 2014 Robert H. Jackson Center National Award for Teaching Justice. He is also the author of *Judging for Themselves: Using Mock Trials to Bring Social Studies and English to Life.*

The Classes They Remember

Using Role-Plays to Bring Social Studies and English to Life

David Sherrin

Routledge
Taylor & Francis Group

NEW YORK AND LONDON

First published 2016
by Routledge
711 Third Avenue, New York, NY 10017

and by Routledge
2 Park Square, Milton Park, Abingdon, Oxon, OX14 4RN

Routledge is an imprint of the Taylor & Francis Group, an informa business

Library of Congress Cataloging-in-Publication Data
Names: Sherrin, David.
Title: The classes they remember: using role-plays to bring social studies and English to life/by David Sherrin.
Description: New York; London: Routledge, [2016] | Includes bibliographical references.
Identifiers: LCCN 2015017542 | ISBN 9781138938687 (hardback) | ISBN 9781138938694 (pbk.) | ISBN 9781315675565 (ebook)
Subjects: LCSH: Simulation games in education. | Role playing. | Social sciences—Study and teaching. | English language—Rhetoric—Study and teaching.
Classification: LCC LB1029.S53 S48 2016 | DDC 371.39/7—dc23
LC record available at http://lccn.loc.gov/2015017542

ISBN: 978-1-138-93868-7 (hbk)
ISBN: 978-1-138-93869-4 (pbk)
ISBN: 978-1-315-67556-5 (ebk)

Typeset in Optima
by Florence Production Ltd, Stoodleigh, Devon, UK

Printed and bound in the United States of America by Publishers Graphics, LLC on sustainably sourced paper.

To Mom and Dad—for always encouraging me to follow my passions and for always believing I would be a writer.

Contents

Companion Website

Rubrics, video examples, templates, and reflection sheets for role-plays can be found on David's website. Go to http://davidsherrin.wix.com/davidsherrin and click on the tab that says "Resources."

Meet the Author

David Sherrin teaches Social Studies and English at Harvest Collegiate in New York City, where he was a founding teacher and is the Social Studies Department Chair. David is also the author of *Judging for Themselves: Using Mock Trials to Bring Learning to Life*. His passion is to engage all students in learning about the complexities of the past through the use of role-playing, mock trials, and the analysis of primary sources.

David was named a New York City Master Teacher for 2014–2015 and was the recipient of the 2014 Robert H. Jackson Center National Award for Teaching Justice. Previously, he taught at the Facing History School and at the Abraham Joshua Heschel School. David spent two years as a street educator for Projeto Axé, a Brazilian organization that provides education and outreach for street children in Salvador, Brazil.

David lives in Brooklyn with his wife, son, and dog. He enjoys cooking, eating well, reading about seventeenth-century Dutch history, and long subway commutes.

Acknowledgments

Early drafts of my work included a number of statements recognizing how my strategies improved due to thoughtful suggestions from my colleagues. This became far too repetitive and so instead, here, I have a more general acknowledgment to some of those who have contributed to this project. Becoming a successful educator in urban public schools and an aspiring writer invariably means that I am surrounded by talented, smart, and caring colleagues. I have learned so much from countless educators throughout my career and New York City is lucky to have such a wealth of great teachers. I could not hope to name all who have contributed to my practice.

So much of my professional achievement in recent years seems to come out of my work with Stephen Lazar, one of the most brilliant (and generous) educators anywhere out there. He has my deepest appreciation and respect. My thanks go out also to the Social Studies Department at Harvest Collegiate—Faye Colon, Andy Snyder, Joshua Vazquez, Andy del-Calvo, and Myles Brawer—for reading early drafts, trying out my strategies, joining in on role-plays, and providing crucial suggestions on scaffolding sheets and strategies for involving the whole class.

I am grateful to members of the English Department—Scott Storm, Zoe Roben, and Beth Krone—for their collaboration in transforming my techniques into use for literature, providing feedback on follow-up discussions, and helping to design relevant literature assessments for role-play.

Thank you to Daniel Braunfeld, a former colleague and currently a program officer at Facing History and Ourselves, for helping to shape my view of what is important to teach in Holocaust education and for feedback on my earliest iterations of role-plays.

My years of experience with role-play could only have come about with the support and encouragement from dedicated and thoughtful administrators. A special thank you to my principal, Kate Burch, for the space she provides for innovation and creativity as well as her critical advice on utilizing primary sources to complement the role-play. I am grateful to the administrators at the Facing History School—Gillian Smith, Dana Panagot, Mark Otto, and Kristina Wylie—who never batted an eye at supporting me in my first attempts at experimenting with this methodology, even when it meant major Spanish–Aztec battles were taking place inside my room. Along those lines, a special thank you to Ahuva Halberstam and Lisa Cohen of the Heschel School for similarly providing me with the room and confidence to find my voice, style, and strategies in my first years of teaching.

I never really understood why many authors thank their editors until I had a chance to partner with Lauren Davis at Routledge. Lauren not only was a pleasure to work with, but she also helped shape the structure of the book by providing big and small suggestions that invariably led to a better product. Thank you for giving just the right support to a first-time author.

Last, a heartfelt thank you to my wonderful family. To my sister Nicki, now a principal, who years ago regaled me with stories of her early years in teaching and surely contributed to my career path. Thank you to my sister, Abby, for giving me the chance many years ago to try my first stabs at storytelling. To my Mom, Dad, and Carol who always made me feel that I chose the right path no matter in which direction it took me. Finally, to my wife Lea, who for more than a decade has patiently sat through dinners sharing in my successes and failures in the classroom, talked over ideas, and joined in trips to pick out props in Chinatown.

Introduction

Playing with Our Minds

Role-playing is a great way to learn how to experience history. It gives us a new perspective on what a person at the time might've been thinking/feeling. I feel like role-playing might be one of the most effective ways to learn and understand history.

(Jade, 11th grader)

The experience of role-playing as a way of learning literature is one that will not be forgotten. Role-playing combined with literature has allowed myself as a student to open myself to new ways of learning. Role-playing has been one of the best techniques I have encountered so far . . . the students still read, but they are also able to put themselves in the characters' shoes, and make decisions that the character would make. Students are also able to understand from the character's perspective.

(Keliza, 11th grader)

These are the classes they remember. In one, a group of students stands atop desks that cross the room. In their mind, it is a bridge taking them out of the city of Tenochtitlan. Other students, sliding on chairs, approach them imagining that they are on canoes gliding across a lake. The room is dark. It is just after midnight. We roll dice, envisioning arrows flying. Some students on the desk are hit and pretend to fall into the cool water below. Those on canoes scoop the prisoners up to bring them back to a temple to offer their hearts in sacrifice.

A second scene: two teenage girls sit on chairs facing each other. In their minds, one is the mother and the other is the daughter. The rest of the class observes. The mother has made a heart-wrenching decision: she will send her child away, on a train transport, to keep her safe from the Nazis. She knows she will likely never see her daughter again. She tries to explain the reason to her daughter. Tears form in their eyes — and in mine. "But don't make me leave you," the daughter cries. "Don't you love me?" "I do," the mother says. "And that is why you need to go even if you don't understand."

Four students stand in the middle of the room. Two of them are playing Juana and Kino, the native Mexican protagonists in a Steinbeck novel who had discovered "the greatest pearl in the world." The other two are buyers who had conspired to low-ball their price. Juana and Kino look desperate. Their future depends on getting the right deal, the one that could guarantee education to their child. Unaware of the pearl's value, they still know that the seller's first offer was a cheat. Kino and Juana's shoulders begin to slump. They argue, their marital unity falling apart in the face of this conflict. And then one seller picks up on the condescending code words of the oppressor: "Just take this deal and go live your little happy lives" he says. We now had our entrance point to talk about race and class in *The Pearl*.

These scenes have something in common. They are all role-plays, in which students became the characters and took ownership of the story before they had learned or read about the outcome. Using prior knowledge and perspective, they took decisions based on the identities and motivations of their characters.

This book is about developing these types of role-plays that bring learning to life. Its roots dig about two decades into the past, well before I had ever contemplated becoming a teacher. I'm going to confess a little something that for years I tried to keep secret. Much of my success as a educator can be traced to that memorable summer of 1992, the one I spent with a bunch of pals sitting on the floor of a friend's living room, mesmerized by the fantastical worlds and adventures created by Mike, his older brother. Mike was in college and we were in middle school so we idolized him. He could not have been any cooler. Little did we know that his immersive world, the universe of Dungeons & Dragons, usually did not exist in the same galaxy as the word "cool." For us, the stories of elves, goblins, and wizards became consuming. The magnetic combination of strategy and luck grabbed us, the sense that we had greater powers but also faced great dangers, that our choices affected our destinies and that we were in it together.

We talked about this alternative reality constantly and not just while we were playing. We argued whether the strongest character was my ranger or another's mage and we craved the next adventure.

I started doing unit-long historical role-plays, first by adapting the strategies of Dungeons & Dragons, about seven years ago, while I was teaching in a high-needs urban school. I was teaching great stories from the past, but the narratives did not consume the students. The classroom seemed to magically transform when I turned it into a D&D laboratory. I read the Dungeon Master guide and broke down the technique to the bare bones, simplifying it to manage with a larger group.

Over the years, my role-play trial strategies developed far beyond the original skeletal structures. After other teachers from my school came to observe the role-playing (and asked "How do I do that in my room?"), I strove to extend the method to other disciplines. My collaboration with English teachers led to a modified technique for role-playing literature. Novels and plays provide at least (if not more) opportunities for such interactive learning, which I have seen from using texts as diverse as *Death of a Salesman, Fences, The Pearl, Of Mice and Men, A Raisin in the Sun,* and *A View from the Bridge.*

This book is a guide for how to create and pull off inspirational role-plays. So many of us, if we truly think back to a memorable educational experience, point to some type of immersion role-play. For me, it was my freshman year in college when I took a class called African Military Conflict and my professor organized a riveting conference simulation about the independence movement in Rhodesia. My hope is that this book will bring this type of powerful experience into your classroom to help deepen your students' understanding and engagement in the class.

Why Should We Do Role-Plays?

Role-playing is interactive education that brings learning to life. Students move around and they feel an emotional tie to the story. It immerses students into history and literature through alternative means beyond the text. Students hear, see, and act the story, increasing their comprehension.

Role-plays cultivate perspective and empathy. Students strive to understand the experiences of others, even if they do not agree with them. Students imagine the narrative, put a text in three dimensions, create alternative scenarios, and see the impact of their choices. One of my students, Julia, explained: "role-playing is helpful in learning history because it puts the students in the shoes of the time period. You can get a much better sense of what the event was like through role-play than you would just from reading about it."

Role-plays help us to make sense of ideas like power, identity, choices and what it means to be human. We look at relationships of power in which stronger groups attempt to exert their power over the "other" for a variety of motives.

This type of learning supports communication and problem solving, whether a group of Aztecs cooperates in responding to the Spanish arrival, Jewish characters secretly plan how to "hide" from the Nazis, or Juana and Kino figure out what to do with the pearl. Role-playing helps students cooperate and then reflect upon the conflict, the stakes, the choices, and the consequences.

I have incorporated role-playing with diverse groups of students. I began them at Facing History School, a public high school in New York City that serves a high-needs population of students. I taught mainly 9th grade and developed these role-plays to support students who were behind grade level.

About three years ago I became one of the founding teachers of Harvest Collegiate, also in Manhattan. Despite its name, Harvest is a regular non-selective public school that takes students from all over the city. Harvest is much more diverse: we have students from low-income and high-needs backgrounds (including about 70 percent free lunch) but we also have a significant cohort of kids from middle- and upper-middle-class families who enter at or above grade level and could easily fit in at prestigious New York City schools. The role-plays serve both of these groups, providing intellectual support and opportunities for extension and inquiry.

Last year, my work as an instructional coach and the chance to teach a Humanities class finally provided the avenue to use role-play for literature. Role-play and most literature coexist naturally: they are both about stories, characters, and conflict. Moreover, the strategy supports literacy as a pre-reading tool. One 11th grader, Zarriah, reflected, "It helps me understand what's happening in the book better . . . It keeps me interested because when we do a role-play I never know if that's going to actually happen in the book. Then I get excited to find out what really happened. It keeps me anxious and in suspense, which is fun to me. Therefore, role-playing is helpful in both learning ways and joyful ways."

By acting out the text first, students gain a deeper understanding of what they will read and a deeper investment in it. Another 11th grader, Mamadou, explained: "In the beginning of the story when we were assigned to read the first couple pages I didn't read at all, then we did the role-play and I really liked it so I decide to actually read, and I enjoyed it . . . I looked forward to the role-play the next day because I knew it would help me understand." Role-playing increases student interest in the story, which has a number of positive consequences. Students are more likely to read, more likely to care about the discussion, and more likely to work on the assessments that build writing skills.

A quiet and shy student named Alberto recognized this dynamic also. He wrote:

This had help me more understanding what is going on the book and a better thinker and role-playing is much fun when it comes to doing writing and acting the part in the book and putting ourselves in the character place and deciding what will they do if they was that character. I also noticed that I had participated a lot more than other books discussions because I can finally understand much better and be afraid more less of getting a wrong answer and having more confident the best class I ever took in my life.

The strategy expands on something many English teachers already do: the read-aloud. In plenty of literature classrooms, teachers support struggling readers by choosing a text with considerable dialogue and rich characters and conflict, selecting students to be the characters, and then having those students read the text aloud. Sometimes they go a step further and "act" out what they are reading. This works particularly well for plays like *Fences* or *Death of a Salesman* since they are mostly dialogue. Teachers may stop periodically for comprehension checks. The goal becomes to use the read-aloud for comprehension before moving on to discuss literary devices and literary analysis. Sometimes the teacher may ask students to make predictions of what happens.

The role-play version does this and more. Students become the characters. When we reach a choice moment we stop reading. We are not only the characters but also the authors. We create the story and the dialogue, based on what we know from the previous text. The effect is that students gain more insight into what the book is really about—its meaning and why it matters.

A strategic use of role-play, along with other resources like film, can have a tremendous impact in supporting literacy. When teaching a difficult text like Victor Hugo's *Les Miserables*, for example, I intertwine the film, role-play, and the book to increase student engagement and comprehension. We begin with the film so that students will grasp the characters and plot, at key moments of tension and conflict we stop the movie to role-play our imagined resolution to the problem, and *then* we read the corresponding section of the book (that we had watched and role-played). Through the book, we discover how the author sets up the conflict and how the characters respond to it. We read past the point that we had watched and role-played to find out the resolution. Only then do we continue with the movie until we reach the following conflict – and the following role-play. The understanding students gain from the movie and role-play makes them want to read the book and it helps them be able to do it effectively.

In both disciplines, immersion expands learners' imagination, empathy, and creativity. One of my students, Nolan, remarked: "I learned that perspectives are important in history. Perspectives affect actions . . . the description of the character's backstories really shape the role-play. Those first scenes really taught me how to analyze 'character' better. Getting into my character was very interesting for me."

The literature role-play functions particularly to get the learners deeply into four key aspects of reading: understanding characters, understanding conflict, evaluating characters' choices, and assessing authorial choices. Charmaine, for example, reflected that:

> Experiencing role-play as a way of learning literature is best for me . . . When we do role-play it help me to better understand the text. Role-playing help you get into the character so you can know and understand what they may be thinking in the next scene or their actions . . . When I read I start to imagine a role-play in my head.

This holds true in Social Studies as well. Most of my historical role-plays are matched with primary sources that tell the same story. Depending on the time period, those sources may use archaic and difficult language. By first acting out the story, students have a greater sense of the overall narrative that they will encounter in the reading and they have more interest in actually reading it. Will the story mesh with the choices they made or tell a different version?

We should not underestimate the importance of the amount of fun and joy that happens in a classroom while role-playing and the subsequent increase in engagement. We laugh and scream in surprise. I remember when one student, playing Louis XVI, attempted to get rid of a document, a few pages long, that would cast suspicion on him as a traitor to the revolution. As I described the mob approaching, he began shoving the paper in his mouth one by one, chewing and swallowing them all to hide the evidence. Nothing I could say would stop him and the room was filled with uproarious laughter at the spectacle.

Role-plays allow all types of students to shine. Those who struggle most in typical settings often become assets in role-plays. The quiet student who carefully takes notes and then provides advice can add something to the scene. The rambunctious child who leaps from his or her seat and can't resist talking (or calling out) can become the star. I have seen students love role-plays who run the gamut from the toughest kids who spend their time in the streets or in the projects to the reclusive gamers who normally don't engage in class but now feel that discussing a "16 in dexterity" speaks to them. Role-plays are a great equalizer against normal socioeconomic and academic inequalities.

This year, for example, two student-created webs of conspiracy ran through my Weimar and Nazi Germany unit. In one, a student named Carlos played a German police officer, a character called Arnold. "Arnold" chose to fire one of his police officers (named "Dirk"). The reason, "Arnold" told me, was because before class he had offered to promote another officer, as a bribe, so that he would hide a Jewish store-owner named "Michael" who had previously helped him out. I agreed, and revealed to the class that neighbors had uncovered Jewish ancestry in Dirk's family and he had been fired. Meanwhile, another student named Darren was playing a German journalist named Julius. He had already decided to use his forgery skill to make false papers to get himself out of Germany. He began to covertly offer his "skill" to Jewish characters and after "Dirk" lost his job "Julius" rolled the dice to forge counterfeit papers showing that Dirk's grandmother was really Aryan.

Darren and Carlos, both 10th graders, were doing extra work and extra thinking to bring the role-play to life. They could not be more different students and outside this class would rarely talk to each other. Darren comes from an upper middle-class family and has a wide-ranging knowledge of history that he often shares in class. He role-plays for fun and carries his own dice with him. He has some organizational and fine-motor difficulties so he does all his schoolwork on a MacBook, which he uses during class. His grades are generally high. Carlos was born in the Dominican Republic. He is charismatic, sharp, and a star when he is on his game, but he rarely was in his first year at the school. He spent considerable time in the dean's office for behavioral and academic problems. He had already failed one of my classes before because he had not handed in any of the work. Now, during the role-play, he had submitted 100 percent of the homework assignments.

With *The Classes They Remember*, I believe that role-plays can become hefty arrows in our pedagogical quivers. I don't always role-play. In a normal semester, I try to have the class engage in one role-play out of the 3–4 main units. There is, of course, so much that we want to accomplish in the classroom that falls outside of what role-plays can do. Most importantly, I want to dedicate time for reading primary and secondary sources, for writing, for research, and for presentations. I hope that this book will help you add a significant new approach to your teaching that can increase student engagement and learning and can complement the other essential work that you do.

After I began writing this book, I discovered an additional reason to celebrate role-playing in middle and high school classrooms: it turns out that a version of historical role-playing called Reacting to the Past (RTTP) is taking college history classrooms by storm. Professor Mark C. Carnes of Barnard College outlines the story behind RTTP and its impact in *Minds on Fire: How Role-Immersion Games Transform College* (Carnes, 2014).[1]

Carnes begins with the simple idea that "Games are play" and that "people enjoy playing." He moves on to explore the ways that role-immersion helps students outperform their peers who are in regular thematic seminars, in every indicator. Role-immersion games, he explains, tap into unused founts of motivation and allow students to take control of the learning, to compete, and to take on roles that challenge their selves and their conception of the world. He also identifies how role-immersion allows students to overcome their own silence, to learn by failing, and to develop a greater sense of empathy and morality. Additionally, research shows that students grow academically because they are more engaged with the textual study that accompanies the role-play.

Now over 350 colleges include RTTP courses based on materials produced by the Reacting Consortium. RTTP, geared toward a more advanced student level, is appropriate for higher education and not for most middle or high schools. Still, the fact that college professors nationwide now choose role-playing to teach history provides yet another layer of support for this pedagogy. And if professors at the college level, who are working with students who are more academically engaged and more mature, are discovering the value of role-playing, imagine what it does for younger learners who need to move around, who need an emotional connection to the content, and who need to feel the experience in order to understand it.

The Structure of this Book

The Classes They Remember: Using Role-Plays and Mock Trials to Bring Social Studies and English to Life places teachers in the process of creating role-play units. It is a recipe for creating role-plays that also has ready-to-go versions that middle school or high school teachers can take and immediately incorporate into their curriculum.

The first chapter explores some common questions that might emerge for teachers before attempting role-plays or after having tried them a few times. My methodologies for role-playing are constantly evolving—each year I try something new that adds an exciting element to the mix. In this section, I discuss issues of structure, student choice, and engagement.

Chapters 2 and 3 provide the template for creating and enacting role-plays together with key scaffolding worksheets. I flesh out the important steps in this process and I include sample scripts of how this would look and sound in reality.

The following section includes ready-to-go units and lessons. My dream is for teachers to take the products of my years of experimentation and implement the units successfully. With this, you can see how something that has been tested and tweaked year after year works in the classroom. You can get the feel of role-play and how to manage it without having to worry about creating one as well.

The first ready-to-go role-play unit evaluates Hernán Cortés, a brilliant but ruthless conquistador who epitomizes the Age of Exploration and Colonization. The role-play transforms students into Spanish, Tlaxcalan, or Aztec individuals in the year 1519. The drama traces the story from the time Cortés and his men receive their mission in Cuba to the downfall of Tenochtitlan. Students make difficult choices, understand the complexity of the encounter, learn why the Spanish conquistadors were able to conquer the Aztec Empire, and determine the most important effects of the conquest.

The next chapter is my Weimar and Nazi Germany role-play, which brings students directly into the question of why the Holocaust happened. Using a veiled allegory of the state of "Nergmay" students delve into the emotions and hardships of Germany after World War I. From there, they make choices while navigating the shifting political landscape in the Weimar Republic and the early years of Nazi Germany. Using an allegorical reality allows students to openly make difficult decisions and to assess them. Students decide who to protect and what matters to them. By the end, they better understand some of the reasons why genocide happens, the roles regular people played, and the impact of their choices on others.

We move into literature role-plays in chapter 6, where we explore the multiple avenues for such learning through texts like *The Pearl, Fences, Death of a Salesman, Of Mice and Men, A View from the Bridge* and *A Raisin in the Sun*. I explain why role-plays are valuable for an English classroom to explore themes and devices like conflict, characterization, and choice. The chapter identifies key choice moments in a number of common novels and plays used in middle and high school classrooms.

The conclusion explores other avenues for role-playing in economics, math, and advisory classes, such as the creation of markets or companies, simulations of hyper-inflation, and economic ideas like factory mass-production, capitalism, and Communism.

Note

1   Carnes, M.C. (2014). *Minds on Fire: How Role-Immersion Games Transform College.* Cambridge, MA: Harvard University Press.

How To Role-Play: A Guide

Common Questions about Role-Playing

I think role-playing really helps you understand why people made the decisions they made. It puts you in the shoes of important people in history and gives you a deeper understanding of complicated eras in history.

(Carlos, 10th grader)

How Do I Keep the Whole Class Engaged and Learning in a Role-Play?

Not every student can act in the role-play at each moment. To keep observers focused on the action and dialogue, and learning from the scenes, I created observer worksheets. Students take an observational role, such as artist, life coach, photographer, or therapist. They watch the role-play using that lens and fill out the corresponding sheet. These sheets actually bring observers indirectly into the action; during pauses we hear from them as they provide insight and advice for the actors. You can find one template on p. 46 and others online.

How Should I Structure the Class and the Classroom?

I utilize three different role-playing structures depending on the needs of a particular scene.

Option 1: The Full-Class Role-Play

The full-class approach works well when every character can be involved, especially during a battle scene. This means orchestrating the action of 20–30 kids shooting arrows, exchanging gifts, or enjoying a banquet. The benefit is that so many students are directly experiencing the action. The drawback can be the logistics of engaging this many students at one time.

Option 2: The Fishbowl Version

In the fishbowl, about 2–10 students role-play in the center of the room and the other students are in a circle around them, actively observing the action and filling out the previously mentioned observer sheets or a rubric for a particular character. During pauses the observers provide advice and do most of the follow-up debrief and reflection.

Option 3: The Small Group Role-Plays

The small-group format works particularly well for English literature role-plays and for historical scenes in which there is a very limited cast of characters. In this structure, you break the class into groups of about 4–5 students. One of them becomes the "master" who gets the script and directs the action. The others take on a character or an observer role. You have 2–5 different groups role-playing the same scene and choice moment at once and you can rotate to observe. Afterwards, as a class you come back to debrief the various ways this played out. In historical scenes, it is particularly interesting when you have many characters making the same type of decision. For example, you can have multiple groups of Jewish families trying to explain to their children what is happening around them.

Can Students Lead Role-Plays?

Yes! Just as in almost any area of teaching, student-led activities add layers of richness to the experience. I particularly enjoy student-led role-plays for literature because the book provides most of the context (instead of the Role-Play Master) so the work is a bit easier. This functions best assuming a few factors: (1) the class has role-played before; (2) we set out the context, conflict, and choices as a larger group; (3) we have a lesson template, observer sheets, and rubrics ready-to-use. The Role-Play Masters must choose moments to pause

Figure 1.1 A Student-Led Scene in Small-Group Format

for reflection and advice, and some suggested questions are available on the template. Once the role-playing process is clear and the context, conflict, and choices of a particular scene are evident, students may also enjoy directing the action. While doing a literature role-play of Arthur Miller's *A View from the Bridge*, one of my students, DJ, took charge by casting the characters, directing the action, leading a debrief, and redoing scenes when needed. At the end, he kicked up his feet and declared, "I need a latte!"

What Do I Do if the Students Want to Change the Story?

Students at times want to do something that is not on the script, but is clearly historically accurate and plausible. For example, I have a scene in which Nazi officers command three teachers to expel their Jewish students. In my script, I assume that the teachers agree to do so under that compulsion and the next scene involves them telling the students. I can't imagine, though, every possible response to the choice. This is, to me, perhaps the most fascinating part of role-play. I can do it every year with students and each time it is legitimately different

5

(if I am doing it right and am opening agency for the students). The students surprise me. While my role-play scripts are highly detailed, I have to be willing to deviate from it and to venture into the unknown along with my students.

This year, in one class a Jewish teacher refused the order and quit her job while the German teacher reluctantly acquiesced. My script called for both the teachers to address the class, but based on their prior decisions only the German teacher did so. In my other class, the two teachers agreed to expel the students, but then conspired to teach them in secret. I allowed them to create a brief plan, they rolled dice for success or failure (they both rolled high and were successful) and then, on the fly, the next scene involved them expelling the students and then revealing their plan to them in secret.

How Accurate Does the Scene Need to Be?

The question of accuracy is important for both historical and literature role-plays. You want to keep everything you provide true to the accepted historical story, especially regarding the places, people, and events that have entered the canon. But then you need to decide where there is wiggle-room for student choice. Let's use an example of a battle between the Spanish and the Aztecs. All the characters are real historical people, some of whom survived the battle and some who did not. For our purposes, it does not matter who survives other than Hernán Cortés and Bernal Diaz del Castillo. It is important that Montezuma not be killed early on and that eventually the Spanish kidnap him. I'm not concerned how they kidnap him and some variation provides interest when we compare their strategy to what is described in the text.

But what do we do if students want to do something totally off the radar and possibly ahistorical? My response has changed over the years. If students asked me to do something far off script during my first attempts at role-plays, I mostly shrugged them off since I didn't have a scene ready and I didn't know whether it had actually happened. Perhaps a student wanted to assassinate Hitler in the Germany role-play or tried to stage a coup against Cortés in the Aztec one.

I've started to realize that my students' instincts in taking on these choices are often right on target with what actually happened and they lead me to learn something new. Usually, I just need to do more research to discover that these choices did take place. There were Germans, including Jews, who did hatch plots to kill Hitler Members of Cortés' crew did try to overthrow him. So now, if a student brings up that option, I may tell him or her to hold off a couple of lessons but I will include that as an option after some research. And when that chance comes, I do frame it within one of the actual attempts to rid Germany of Hitler.

What Do I Do if a Key Student Isn't There to Play Her Role?

There are days when an incredibly well-planned scene will need last-minute reshuffling because a student with a key role is absent or no student ever chose that character in the first place.

This is an example of where you just need to be light on your feet in managing the scene. Think of the big picture of what you want to get out of that scene and move some pieces around to get there. For example, my Germany role-play involves a book-burning scene in which two Jews, Simon and Rachel, stumble across a group of Germans throwing books authored by Jews into the pile. Simon is a history professor and in the lesson's background I state that Rachel's brother also wrote some of the books. I want to get at both the personal and communal nature of this conflict they find themselves in.

This year, no student had chosen to play Simon and, unfortunately, Rachel was absent. This is a typical dilemma, especially when you have the fortune of a small class (interestingly, a really small class can be a boon in every sense except, sometimes, in role-play). I needed to replace them with other similar characters. For Rachel, pretty much any Jewish female could function. To replace Simon, it made sense to put in Joshua, the rabbi, as he could easily have written a book about Judaism that was also in the pile. The shift in characters took about 30–60 seconds to work out and we were ready-to-go.

What Do We Do if We Don't Finish the Role-Play?

A sense of pacing helps role-plays function, but it only really comes from experience. There are certainly times when I do not finish the established "lesson" in one of my role-plays whether because a scene was too compelling to stop or due to student interruptions (yes, that happens to me too!).

To resolve this, I need to weigh the importance of what we missed. If necessary, we can start the next day by finishing that scene and truncating the following ones. Other times, we skip the second or third scene from that lesson and I just add a brief description of what we missed to the background narrative the following day.

Start off making your daily goal small and manageable. If I include three scenes in a particular lesson of a role-play, try to do the one or two that you think are most important. Another year try something else. We often get so caught up attempting to get it "perfect" that we lose sight of the larger goals. The minor details of every role-play are less crucial than the overall understandings and experiences.

Are there Different Types of Role-Plays?

There are many ways to enact role-plays, especially if you begin to develop mock trials, diplomacy, economic, or math role-plays. Here, though, I will focus on what I call imaginative or participatory. The former is the style most often used in a traditional Dungeons & Dragons setting. In this case, the students sit, perhaps in a circle, and the students and teacher describe all of the actions verbally. Everything, in a sense, takes place in our heads. We describe movements, dancing, and sword thrusts. There is an advantage in this in that it keeps the class composed and a bit more orderly.

At a certain point, you may decide, as I did, to open the box and allow for fully participatory role-playing in which students are up and out of their chairs. They are physically acting out the scenes. They may be marching across a room, mimicking a human sacrifice, or dancing. They might pull desks together to create a fortress, launch a catapult, or even stick someone's head under a cardboard guillotine.

What Should Your Newly Created Role-Play Look Like?

When you compose your own role-play, consider what you need to make it work and what the students need. For this book's samples, I put extra attention into every detail so that others can use them. For myself, I need much less.

Your role-plays should get better and more detailed over time. In my first years I did not provide fully fleshed-out character descriptions (only names and jobs, such as "Robert, Jewish butcher"). I didn't have Pivotal Discussion Debates. My limited homework assignments connected to the role-play's content but they were not fully integrated. The students had fewer avenues for choice. I didn't have terms like "choice moments" or even speaking cards. I just mostly told them what to say when needed. The steps I have now make the role-plays better but my incipient versions were still dynamic, thought provoking, and energizing. They were still the highlights for my students and the classes they talked about when they visited from college. It is okay not to get "perfection" in your first attempts.

What Do I Do if the Emotions or Language Seem Inappropriate to the Classroom?

One question that we all must consider when developing a role-play is how to prepare students intellectually and emotionally for the content, especially when getting into topics like Germany's treatment of Jews under Nazi rule. It is useful to remind them that these are events that real people lived through. For the most part, I've found role-plays cultivate more empathy for the tribulations of individuals than almost any other type of teaching. Students might actually say "This is so sad; I can't do this." It is, in a sense, the definition of empathy to put ourselves in the emotional positions of others.

Along that vein, we might question what is appropriate for students to say in a role-play. I've found that issue to be most salient in the Germany role-play. For the story to function not everyone can be "good" and say the things we want to hear. For me, using the allegories of "Nergmay," "Wejs" and "Sizans" instead of "Germany," "Jews," and "Nazis" provides the freedom for students to make real choices and to create a true scenario without feeling the (rightful) pressure to be sensitive to higher morality. As one of my students, Julia, explained: "separating Nergmay and Germany is helpful because it removes the students from the event so that there's not really space for any real anti-Semitism, but the students can still experience a parallel of Nazi Germany." Certainly, I feel better for a student to say "I don't want Wejs to be here" than "I don't want Jews to be here," even if we know it is just a lightly veiled allegory.

How Should I Communicate My Role-Play Intentions to my Administration and/or Parents?

Some role-plays might include sensitive material and, depending on the realities of your school and district, you might want to check in with concerned stakeholders about your plans. I'm thinking here, specifically, about the Weimar and Nazi Germany role-play. I have had the fortune to always work with supportive and innovative administrators who trusted my judgment, but not every teacher does. It also helped that my grandparents were Holocaust survivors, which certainly may assuage any possible concern about my intentions or sensitivity in developing and implementing a role-play about Nazi Germany. If you are doing such a role-play for the first time, especially one involving human rights abuses, it would be valuable to speak with your administrators and possibly send a letter or email to parents explaining what will be taking place and your reasons why.

CHAPTER

2

Creating Role-Plays

Every time I role-play I have fun and it's really interesting to see how the other students think about the topic that we are learning about. I also think it helps students to speak up more and not be so afraid to speak which can prepare us for work that we have to do in the future.

(Sophia, 10th grader)

I think that role-playing is a great way to enhance learning in a fun and educational environment. I feel as if role-playing is a great hands on experience to learning, it's very enticing to see how people will react from certain situations. The best thing about role-playing is that it's something we can pick up on the next day and be excited to. I would recommend this type or style of teaching to all history teachers in order for the students to be entertained and to be mentally and physically engaged with the classroom.

(Matthew, 10th grader)

The Process

This chapter provides an outline for you to create historical and literature role-plays. Some of the steps are necessary only for historical units since in literature the author has done much of our work for us: the characters are there, the scenes are there, the book, itself, is the background narrative. The dialogue becomes the action cards. I think the rich language takes away the necessity for props; the literature creates the setting and the imagery.

There are countless historical events and great works of literature for you to consider that lend themselves to role-playing, with the following being a few great examples.

Table 2.1 Suggestions for Role-Play Topics and Texts

Historical Role-Plays	Literature Role-Plays
The Cuban Missile Crisis	*The Pearl*
The Roaring Twenties	*Of Mice and Men*
American Labor Movements	*Raisin in the Sun*
The Indian Removal Act	*Fences*
Westward Expansion	*A View from the Bridge*
Vietnam War Protests	*The Crucible*
Feminism	*Bodega Dreams*
The Rise and Fall of the Berlin Wall	*Lord of the Flies*
Ordinary People in the Revolutionary War	*Romeo and Juliet*
The Russian Revolution	*Les Misérables*

There are a number of steps for developing a new role-play that I discuss in this section: selecting a story; researching; creating (or determining) the characters; determining the scenes; writing the background narratives; deciding on conflicts and choice moments; creating action and speaking cards; gathering props; determining homework assignments; pivotal decision debates; creating an assessment.

Selecting a Story

For an historical role-play, we need an event that has a gripping story, historical importance, abundant conflict, and a large cast of characters who are involved in most events. They might be famous individuals, regular people, or archetypes of typical individuals from the time and place.

Choosing a story for a literature role-play is almost as difficult as choosing a text for your class, in the sense that the main frustration is having too many options. Once you take into consideration issues like the difficulty of the text, the interests of your students, and the larger themes of your course, you can consider whether specific texts work for role-playing. Since this strategy works best in the realm of characterization and conflict, your main criteria should be whether the book has complex characters, at least three or four difficult choices that the characters must make, and moments of conflict (hopefully between the characters) that match up with those choices.

In either discipline, the right story has physical, verbal, or emotional conflict between the characters as well as moments of moral ambiguities and difficult choices. If it is easy to make the decisions, then it is not worth role-playing. I want to put the students in situations where they decide to act in ways that they are unhappy about in order for their characters to survive or thrive.

Researching (Historical Role-Plays Only)

To create a role-play you need to research primary and secondary sources. I start with one or two secondary sources that lay out the narrative arc. This allows me to identify 8–12 scenes that form the backbone of the unit. For example, the book *The Days of the French Revolution* breaks down the revolution into about ten days, each of which is a chapter. Those ten days each became separate lessons for my unit.

Primary sources like *Broken Spears* and *The Discovery and Conquest of Mexico* provide key details, including character identities and dialogue, which I can add into a role-play with my action or speaking cards. Excerpts of these sources may also become the homework assignments. Role-plays should not exist independently of a larger curriculum in which students are reading, analyzing, sourcing, and corroborating historical texts.

Creating (or Determining) the Characters

For literature, there is certainly no need to create the characters; the author has done the work for us and likely created characters that have depth, nuance, and complex identities far beyond what we could accomplish on our own. We just need to determine which characters are relevant to each conflict and choice moment so we know who will be in the role-play scene. I use the chart at the end of this section to keep track of that information.

In literature we will likely only encounter five or so principal individuals. This is not a problem; it just means that we perform fewer full-class role-plays and instead focus on fishbowl or small-group scenes. Meanwhile, we must have about 25–30 characters for an historical role-play. In literature role-plays, we switch who plays the protagonists each day. In historical ones, students are the same characters throughout the whole unit.

During my research reading, I jot down the names and positions of key individuals. In the Aztec–Spanish encounter, all the Spanish characters' names and jobs are accurate. When possible, I included real Aztecs or Tlaxcalans who lived through this event. I couldn't find enough names of real Tlaxcalans, so I looked up common indigenous names from Mexico and then created jobs for them based on the needs of the role-play.

For my French Revolution unit, the extensive availability of sources meant that I could ensure that every character was a true historical person ranging from the king and members of his court to bakers, grocers, and flower sellers.

The characters for the Weimar and Nazi Germany role-play are all archetypal ordinary people to keep the experience allegorical. No one is playing Hitler or Himmler. The story is about choices that regular people made.

Here is an example of one fully fleshed-out character description. Note the key elements such as age, job, outlook, family life, and a success mission:

> **Pedro de Alvarado, Second-in-Command**—You are a 34-year-old captain, second-in-command to Cortés. You are loyal to Cortés but you have a different vision. While Cortés values diplomacy and alliance-building you favor war. You mistrust natives and look down upon them. You would prefer to gain power by destroying the opposition. Your wife, Teresa, died two years before and your sadness, perhaps, explains your anger toward people you view as enemies. Your success mission is to find a way to take over the Aztec capital by force to secure your name in history, to defeat them in battle, and to use it as a stepping stone for further conquests in the region.

Determining the Scenes

Each role-play lesson includes 1–3 scenes, which are the contexts that surround those points in which characters make key decisions or actions. Examples of scenes include the establishment of the Spanish–Tlaxcalan alliance, Mama and Walter Jr. debating what to do with the insurance money, or the Nazi boycott of Jewish-owned stores.

Scenes are the larger tapestries upon which we stitch various threads of the role-play: the background narrative, the dialogue (using speaking cards), the conflict and choice moments, the actual role-playing, and the pauses for analysis, advice, and reflection.

In the Weimar Unemployment and Labor Strikes lesson, for example, there are three scenes: (1) a brief meeting between unemployed characters in which a plot is hatched; (2) the action scene in which some characters attempt to break the picket; (3) the negotiation with the factory boss. The background narrative sets the context by explaining the post-World War I tension in Germany, the increased unemployment, and the labor strikes. A speaking card in which one character suggests that they might break a picket to gain jobs establishes the internal conflict and the choice moment. The subsequent role-playing involves the students enacting their choices and interacting with the characters on strike.

In an historical unit we act out enough scenes to tell a fleshed-out version of the story. Literature role-plays involve enough scenes with conflicts and choice moments to fill out 6–10 days of role-playing. You may not want to role-play every major conflict, instead interweaving the immersion with close reading, seminar discussions, and other effective pedagogies. In literature, we can pick and choose more easily which scenes we want to just read and which we want to role-play. When I taught *The Pearl*, for example, I identified 12 key choice moments. When it came to putting together the unit, however, I chose to role-play only 6 of those scenes, with three of them mostly bunched together into one lesson.

Writing the Background Narratives (Historical Role-Plays Only)

The background provides the context for the role-play and sets the stage for a scene, conflict, and a choice moment. The background answers crucial questions: When is this taking place? Where is this taking place (the setting)? What are the details that explain why the events are about to happen? What are the typical emotions and thoughts of the population at that time? What happened between the previous scene and this one?

In my first Aztec–Spanish role-play lesson, I write: "Those of you who are Spaniards are on the beach of Cuba. It is a white, sandy beach. The day is hot, the sun burns on your skin." This is to highlight the visceral sensations and to put the students imaginatively into the scene. I also use the background to fill in gaps in the story that we do not have time to role-play. For instance, in a later lesson I write: "The Spanish almost immediately get into battles with smaller Mexican tribes that live by the water. Using their guns, steel armor, and horses, the few Spanish troops are able to defeat much larger armies with very few losses. The Spanish receive some gifts from this tribe, including some of the Tabascan women. One of them is named Malinche. The Spanish baptize her and call her Dona Marina. She speaks many of the local languages and quickly learns Spanish. She becomes Cortés' interpreter."

Background narratives, written in student-friendly language, should be concise. In my planning, I make sure to include a comprehension check—a few quick questions to ensure students have grasped the essential background for the role-play.

Deciding on Conflicts and Choice Moments

Choice moments are when one or more individuals in the role-play make a key decision, often ethical, that will drive the subsequent acting and action. They involve the characters' need to navigate through interior or exterior conflicts. Choice moments normally result from a particular prompt in the background or from the speaking cards that have set up a conflict. The outcomes are entirely up to the students, although we, as the guides, may question them to push them in a specific direction. Every role-play lesson must have 1–3 choice moments.

Choice moments are the fulcrums upon which the entire role-play rests. The background and speaker cards develop the context for a rich choice moment, many of which require choosing between competing values or cases in which characters are in conflict with someone they care about. These times of tension may force characters to decide between their own safety or professional success, or between prioritizing their family's well-being or helping a stranger in need.

In literature, an important task is identifying exactly where the choice moment is and exactly at what point do we stop the students from reading so that they grasp the conflict but do not know the book's resolution, thereby leaving the opportunity for an open role-play.

There is a give-and-take relationship between conflicts and choices. Conflicts create choices and vice versa. For example, the increasing level of conflict between the Aztecs and Spanish forces both sides to make tough choices, but then the resulting choices inevitably lead to further conflict. I've noticed that most, but not all, of my role-play conflicts and choice moments tend to fall under six categories that are not mutually exclusive: negotiation, strategic planning, intrafamilial conflict, ethical dilemmas, individual physical or verbal conflicts, and battles.

Negotiations might include trying to get a job, attempting to gain an exit visa to leave Germany, or a meeting between Spanish–Aztec ambassadors. Strategic planning could be figuring out how to kidnap Montezuma or what the best option is for the Jewish community after *Kristallnacht*. Examples of intrafamilial conflicts are when Kino and Juana argue over what to do with the pearl, when parents try to convince their children not to join the Hitler Youth, or when a parent explains to a child why she has to leave on a *kindertransport*. Ethical dilemmas abound in role-plays, such as what to do during a book burning, whether or not to hide Jews, and who to help during a smallpox epidemic. Individual conflicts include scenes during *Kristallnacht* and encounters between Jews and the Hitler Youth. Lastly, battle scenes take place often between the Spanish and Aztec armies at various points during that role-play.

Within these conflicts, the key points are the choice moments, which I identify in my ready-to-go units as follows.

Choice Moment 2 (Spanish characters)

Governor Velazquez wants you to turn back. What do you do?

Here are some examples of choice moments:

- *Encounter in the Americas*: What should the Aztecs do about having a kidnapped king who is collaborating with the Spanish soldiers?
- *Weimar and Nazi Germany*: Should a Jewish mother tell the truth to her child about why he is being kicked out of school or lie to him?
- *The Pearl*: Should Juana steal the pearl from Kino to try to save her family?

Creating Action and Speaking Cards (Historical Role-Plays Only)

Action and speaking cards help strike the balance between providing students freedom of choice and guiding them toward specific conflicts and actions that are historically accurate. For example, I use a speaking card to require Cortés to insult the Aztec religion in order to ensure that the event takes place and then to give Montezuma a choice moment in how to respond. Whenever possible, consult a reliable primary source to try to use a character's actual language in the card. Here is an example of what a speaking card looks like:

Card 3F (Member of 3rd Estate)

"We want the Bastille! Out with the troops!"

Gathering Props

If you are doing a kinesthetic role-play, props are optional but can add a wonderful element. Sometimes props are actual specimens or poor imitations of the objects being used. I bring in plastic swords, a felt crown, and robes. I always have a wig handy. For an Aztec–Spanish banquet, I supply real food for us to eat (like chocolate and salsa) and some symbolic food to exchange, such as a bag of dried rice. There are times when I simply print out pictures of something like a chicken or a cereal box to be purchased or exchanged. Even I'm not ready to bring in a live chicken to increase authenticity.

Props are not necessary for a literature role-play but they may be helpful. In *The Pearl*, I spontaneously grabbed a bottle of glue for one scene to represent the pearl and one of my students snagged a baseball glove for her to coddle as if it were her baby, Coyotito.

Determining Homework Assignments

In my role-plays, we always act out the event before reading the sources or book to discover the "true" story. The students thus have more freedom to make their choices based on their understanding of the context and their characters because they are not influenced by what they know to have happened. The subsequent homework covers the same scenes and tells the same story. In English classes, given that many pages often separate the choice moments, one obvious assignment is to ask students to read the intervening pages, stopping one or two pages short of the next conflict. We usually spend about 10–15 minutes the next day discussing the homework.

For social studies, historical reading that matches up with the role-play is essential both to cultivate literacy and because reading is at the center of the discipline. Moreover, while the role-playing helps build comprehension we also want to make sure to "check" what we did in class against the historical record. Lastly, by using competing sources that provide alternative views of the events, we can further build students' grasp of sourcing and historical perspective.

I have experimented with many types of homework assignments, all in the somewhat hallucinatory vision that I can get a large percentage of my students to complete them. My go-to assignments have always been readings that match up with the scenes of that day, complement the role-plays, and lead to discussions about discrepancies between what we chose to do in class and what "actually" happened according to the source.

Each year, I managed to add new elements to the reading list. For example, in the Encounters in the Americas I began with primary source readings from the Aztec perspective but a few years ago I integrated a dual assignment that also had the students look at Bernal Diaz del Castillo's book, which provides a Spanish conquistador's view. As I have increased the amount of text, it also became important to increase my differentiation to support my spectrum of students by creating various levels through adaptation and excerpts. Each night, I have two levels of readings; students choose from either as they come through the door. Level A includes excerpts from the original texts. Level B, which I call the "slightly easier version," includes an excerpted and adapted text.

Part of me, however, always wanted students to write daily perspective pieces since the role-plays provide such a vivid spark to ignite diary entries from the point-of-view of the characters. In the past few years, in my historical units I've melded the reading and writing options by having students read shorter primary sources and then write diary entries as their characters responding to the day's events and to the sources. We discuss ways to make it seem like the character actually encountered what is in the source: perhaps he is in the picture, or took the photograph, or visited a friend's house and saw the scene, or saw the image in the newspaper.

These diary entry reflections serve many purposes, including allowing students to reflect on that day's events and to prepare for upcoming pivotal decision debates (PDDs) by developing their thinking on a particular issue. Notice how in the following homework assignment, Figure 2.1, Michelle creatively integrates four sources into her character's understanding of *Kristallnacht*, the night's meaning for Jews, and her prediction of what will happen.

In this book, for each of the example historical role-plays, I have included the homework writing prompt as well as the sources I use. As you begin to develop your own style, experiment whether you want to focus on the reading (perhaps with an annotation strategy), the writing, or both. When creating your own role-plays, think about the types of sources (including photographs) that will illuminate the larger ideas from the scenes you enacted in class.

There are a few small moves that you can make that have positive ripple effects, such as providing "character points" regularly or periodically for students who complete homework assignments. It is fascinating to observe that many students care more about making their character stronger than about their own grade!

For English classes, there are also myriad opportunities for writing. With characterization, choice, and conflict being so central to this strategy, I have leaned toward asking students to write a diary entry from one character's

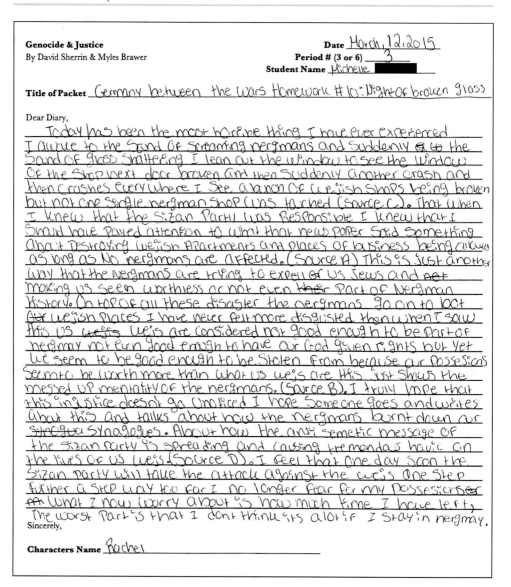

Genocide & Justice
By David Sherrin & Myles Brawer

Date March, 12, 2015
Period # (3 or 6) ___3___
Student Name Michelle ▮▮▮▮

Title of Packet Germany between the Wars Homework #10: Night of broken glass

Dear Diary,

Today has been the most horrible thing I have ever experienced I awoke to the Sand of Screaming nergmans and suddenly the Sand of glces Shattering I lean out the window to see the window of the Shop next door broken and then Suddenly another crash and then crashes everywhere I see a bunch of cuejish Shops being broken but not one Single nergman Shop was harmed (Source C). That when I knew that the Sizan Party was Responsible I knew that I Should have payed attention to what that news paper Said something about Destroying cuejish Apartments and places of business being allowed as long as No nergmans are affected. (Source A) This is just another way that the Nergmans are trying to expell of Us Jews and not making us seem worthless or not even their part of Nergman History. On top of all these disaster the nergmans go on to loot for cuejish places I have never felt more disgusted than when I saw this us cuejis cuejis are considered not good enough to be part of nergmay not even good enough to have our God given rights but yet We seem to be good enough to be Stolen from because our possesions Seem to be worth more than what us cuejis are this just shows the messed up meniafity of the nergmans. (Source B). I truly hope that this injustice doesn't go unnoticed I hope Some one goes and writes about this and talks about how the nergmans burnt down our streets synagogues. About how the anti semetic message of the Sizan Party is spreading and causing tremendas havic on the lives of us cuejis (Source D). I feel that one day Soon the Sizan Party will take the attack against the cuejs one step further a Step way too far I no longer fear for my possesions or What I now worry about is how much time I have left, The worst Part's that I don't think its alot if I Stay in nergmay.

Sincerely,

Characters Name Rachel

Figure 2.1 Michelle's "Night of Broken Glass" Homework

perspective. Students should focus on the character's view of his or her choices in the book, a reflection on the consequences, and predictions on the future. Students can choose a character and write a diary explaining his or her perspective on the scene we enacted. They can write out their imaginary version of the next scene. If a homework reading leads up to a conflict moment, then the student can finish the reading, choose a character, and write an entry or letter explaining what he or she should do in that conflict. If you're looking for a more analytical bent, students can read the author's text and then write a comparison between the role-play and the actual text and why the writer made those choices.

Pivotal Decision Debates (Historical Role-Plays Only)

In historical role-plays, each lesson and the accompanying homework assignments lead up to what I call "Pivotal Decision Debates" (PDD). These are moments in which members of the community gather to discuss a question whose resolution will have great bearing on their future. This is distinct from "choice moments" which are often individual in nature and usually require coming to a quick decision. These PDDs add additional skill-building elements to the role-playing toolbox by incorporating students' growing knowledge, their perspective of their roles, and their use of evidence from homework texts into a debate.

Each of my units contains two or three of these pivotal decision debates. The Weimar and Nazi Germany role-play, for instance, includes a PDD on the 1932 election and another on choices that the Jewish and German communities must make after the Nazis begin state-sanctioned persecution of the Jews. The Spanish–Aztec encounter role-play includes PDDs about whether the Tlaxcalans should ally with the Spanish and how Aztec and Spanish leaders should respond to growing tension.

The format of each PDD plays out and depends on the political context of that community. In some cases, an autocratic leader like Cortés might hear the different options and then make the decision. In others, like a French Revolution role-play, there could be a vote. Depending on whether you turbo-boost your role-plays, and whether or not you keep track of character points as a way to incentivize students, the ability to "win" a PDD could lead to extra character points and new powers.

Creating an Assessment

I assess students' participation in the role-play and their learning in a role-play unit, generally, in four ways: rubrics that assess the actual role-play, quizzes, in-class writing, and projects. These should all work in tandem. Role-plays should help illuminate what students understand before the writing so that we can target certain skills and knowledge prior to the end-of-unit assessments.

Many students put every ounce of their being into the role-plays. They become their characters and they strive to make decisions that are authentic to the characters' identities, to their missions, and to the context around them. Oftentimes, these are students who do not shine elsewhere and so, among other reasons, I believe we should assess the students on their role-play performance itself. I've included in our online resources two examples of rubrics to help with this. The first is one that I created based on four learning goals: responsibility, perspective, context and comprehension, and voice. A class of students created the second rubric after having experienced a number of days of role-playing. Among a list of standards, they chose to build the rubric around context, perspective and voice, creative contribution, and connections. The wording of the indicators is mostly theirs, with some slight adjustments on my part. I also included a simple self-evaluation rubric that can be handy for daily or periodic use.

Quizzes serve for assessing content knowledge of an historical unit or a novel. Many students who normally struggle with content excel at remembering information and understanding big ideas when they learn it through role-play. Students recognize this. Alex, a 10th grader, wrote: "We learn a lot of inform-ation that would not stick with us if we were being lectured all the time, and we also are able to realize emotion, scenery, and knowledge . . . This helps us realize so much about not only history but also people and how to interact." A quiz during or after role-play can serve as a reward and a boost for students because their grade on that test will likely be the highest of the year.

An in-class writing task is valuable for students who do not regularly complete homework assignments or projects, allowing us to grasp where they are and what they are learning. At my school, we call these assessments "benchmark tasks." We provide the students with a question like "Why did the Nazi Party gain power in Germany in 1932?" and with four or five primary or secondary sources, each about one page-length. Students have one day to read and annotate, and a second day to write an essay. This assessment allows us to gauge their understanding of a major question of the role-play unit, their ability to glean sources for evidence, and their skill at writing essays with clear claims and supporting evidence.

For me, however, deep learning is missing something when it does not include an authentic project or performance task. What do the students *do* with their learning?

I've developed a number of projects, each of which produces thoughtful student work. One option that ties in perfectly with the larger unit is to ask students to make a portfolio of their three or four strongest diary responses.

Students can choose to revise and strengthen them, and they should create an introduction and/or conclusion (from their character), explaining why their individual story and the larger history are important to be heard.

At times, I've provided students with a "menu" of choices. One option could be the above "diary entry" portfolio. Another is a traditional essay that answers an essential question. In literature, you may focus on literary elements that are central to role-playing, such as characterization and conflict. You might consider asking them to choose a conflict in the book and to discuss what led to that conflict and what is at stake for the characters at that moment. Another option is to ask students to discuss how the author uses literary elements like conflict and characterization to create tension in the text.

A third choice in the menu is for students to make a memorial sculpture for someone like Cortés or a protagonist in a novel. This needs to be an actual three-dimensional clay piece that includes an artist statement. This past semester, for example, Oliver made a wonderful sculpture depicting Cortés as a villain with a flowing cape and Aztec heads at his feet.

Depending on the case study of your role-play, another wonderful assessment is a mock trial in which you put one of the characters (or a related historical figure) on trial. For example, we follow-up with our Nazi Germany role-play by putting Julius Streicher on trial. The mock trial becomes an assessment of their learning during the unit and also an extension activity. The students build on their overall understanding of the Holocaust but they must address a new situation and new primary sources to do it. It is also worth thinking about whether you could do a trial of any character in a particular novel or play using the strategies that I outline in my book about mock trials, *Judging their Learning*. You could put George on trial for killing Lenny, using only the evidence from the book. What is his defense?

Finally, a creative literature project option that aligns closely with the ethos of role-playing is to ask students to choose a scene in the book with a choice moment and to imagine the character making another choice. At that point, the students must rewrite the following pages with the consequences of that choice and other characters' reactions, basing the decisions on what he or she knows of the characters. You may want to ask the student to include a separate reflection explaining the choices and how (s)he supports them based on previous actions of the characters. Similarly, you might ask students to write the next few pages after the end of the book, using equivalent criteria.

Template for History Role-Play Lesson

Topic/title: _____

Background narrative:

_____

_____

_____

_____

_____

_____

_____

_____

Comprehension Checks:

What are three important pieces of information from the background?

1. _____

2. _____

3. _____

The Gist:

Today the students . . .

_____

_____

By the end, the students must . . .

_____

_____

Homework

Compelling Question: _____

_____

Source	Title or Author
A.	
B.	
C.	
D.	
Extension secondary source	

Warm-up:

_____

_____

Scene 1: _____

Scenery:

_____

_____

_____

Role-players:

_____

_____

_____

Teacher reads:

Speaking card 1 ( ): _____

_____

Speaking card 2 ( ): _____

_____

Choice moment 1 ( ): _____

- What do you do?

_____

Choice moment 2 ( ): _____

- What do you do?

_____

Students will roll dice if they:

_____

_____

An outcome I cannot live with is if:

_____

_____

Pause questions (choose one or more):

- What are the stakes at this moment for these characters?
- What are the characters' options?
- What advice and thoughts can our "therapists" and "life coaches" give?
- Why is this a difficult decision?
- Why is your character making this choice?
- How realistic is the character's choice so far based on her identity and the situation?

Additional Actions/Speaking after Pause

Speaking card 3 ( ): _____

_____

Speaking card 4 ( ): _____

_____

Choice moment 3 ( ): _____

- What do you do?

_____

Reflection and debrief (choose one or more):

- What was one emotion that you imagine the characters felt? Why?
- How did the characters interact with each other?
- Were the characters' choices realistic? Why or why not?
- What was the meaning of this role-play? Why did the scene matter?
- What is one thing you wonder?

A Lesson Template for Literature Role-Play

Pre-planning

Page # of conflict: _____

Brief description of conflict: _____

_____

_____

_____

Characters involved: _____

_____

_____

_____

Fishbowl or small-group format: _____

_____

_____

Set-up

Students will read until page #: ____

Questions to establish background, context, and conflict (choose one or more):

- What do we need to know about the story? What is the situation?
- What do we need to know about the characters and their relationships?
- What is the conflict? What are the stakes of this conflict?
- What is the "choice moment?"

We will take this role-play until _____

_____

_____

Assigning the roles:

Character 1 (   ) will be played by _____

Character 2 (   ) will be played by _____

Character 3 (   ) will be played by _____

Character 4 (   ) will be played by _____

Beginning the role-play:

Where will the actors be stationed?

_____

_____

_____

_____

Who will begin? _____

My prompt sentence to start is: _____

Pauses (choose one or more):

- What are the characters thinking?
- What advice do you have for them?
- Are their actions realistic?
- What prior clues in the text can help us decide their choices?
- What are their options?

Debrief (choose one or more):

- What predictions can we make about how the author will write this scene?
- What themes does this role-play reveal?
- What is the meaning of this scene? Why does it matter?
- What do we think the characters would do after this scene?

Table 2.2 Assigning Roles for Group Role-Play

Role	Student
RP Master	
Character 1 _____	
Character 2 _____	
Character 3 _____	
Character 4 _____	
Therapist	
Artist	
Life coach	
Rubric scorer for _____	
Rubric scorer for _____	
Rubric scorer for _____	
Rubric scorer for _____	

CHAPTER

3

Executing Role-Plays

In this chapter, I outline how to put role-plays into action. In my 47-minute period, I try to use about 20–25 minutes for the role-play. I divide the rest between a warm-up, homework discussion, and debrief. For me, a general outline of a role-play lesson includes the following steps. The actual role-play begins at step 5 and continues until step 13.

1. Students walk in and take the homework assignment and observation sheet.
2. Warm-up: A reflective question, review questions, or brief reading (meanwhile I hand out any speaking cards or prompts).
3. Warm-up discussion.
4. Homework discussion.
5. Reading of background and comprehension check.
6. Setting the scene.
7. Develop the conflict with introduction, speaking cards, and first actions.
8. Identifying a choice moment; defining the stakes and options.
9. Role-play of choice moment.
10. Pausing for analysis.
11. Reaction: Role-playing again, continuing the scene, or trying out more than one option.
12. Repeat of steps 6–10 with a new scene and choice moment (optional).
13. Final debrief.

The chart below shows a typical flow of a scene once the role-playing has begun.

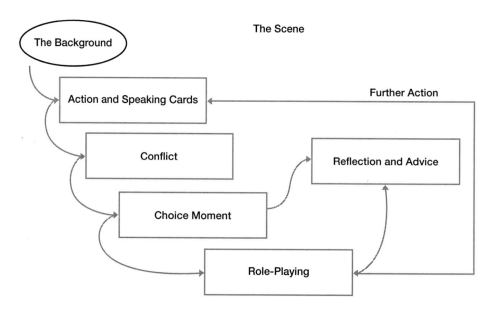

Figure 3.1 The Role-Play Flow

Prior to the Class

For social studies classes, I print out two copies of the script. I hang on to one to use during class and I use the second copy to cut out the speaking cards to give to students. In either discipline, I place the homework and observation sheets in an accessible spot for students. If I'm using props, I'm sure to have them at hand as well.

Warm-up

Warm-up activities provide a meaningful start while allowing you to handle some logistics, such as attendance. With role-plays, this is time for additional teacher tasks like handing out props or speaking cards, assigning characters, or checking in with a student about a character's situation.

Whether history or English, it is helpful to utilize the warm-up to bring students back to the central themes and elements of the story. You might take this time to discuss meaning, connections to the world, issues of identity, and/or connections to self. For example, "describe a time when you or others you know were singled out and treated differently because of who they were."

One effective warm-up strategy is the thought-provoking essential question—something like "Based on what you've seen so far, is Hernán Cortés a hero or a villain?" or "What is the role of race and class in *The Pearl*?" These questions push students to reflect on key ideas of the unit. Another example: one day I might ask the students, "What are the choices that Jews have in Germany after the *Kristallnacht*?"

I also use warm-ups for quick content review, whether through a vocabulary-matching exercise, putting events in chronological order, or four quick comprehension questions. This allows for spiraling, or circling back to earlier content to ensure that it stays in the students' minds.

The final way that I do warm-up is by starting students on their homework reading, which provides an incentive for them to finish it at home. Perhaps it is because they have seen that they can do it or because they are more likely to remember to do it later. Some teachers give homework time at the end of class, but my colleagues and I have observed that students focus more on reading at the beginning of class.

Warm-up Discussion

Pacing is difficult in role-play units because with students highly engaged in the topic, they want to discuss it more. A thought-provoking warm-up question that ties into their scenes can eat up most of the period. Make the structure of this discussion, and its limitations in terms of time or number of speakers, clear from the outset, otherwise, you might not get to that role-play.

Homework Discussion

For literature classes, a homework debrief should combine any of your go-to moves for close literary analysis along with an overall plot summary. The role-play should be there to complement your larger learning goals not to overwhelm them, so the major themes and close reading of the text should not go unexplored. The plot and character summary from the homework is essential, though, to keep all students up to speed and thereby engaged in the story so that they can participate actively in the upcoming role-plays. There is a domino effect; involvement in the role-plays stimulates interest to complete the homework readings and vice versa.

In either discipline, I begin with the students' responses: What are their questions? What did they find interesting or surprising? Then, we move on to analysis: How was the text(s) we read similar or different from the previous day's role-play?

In social studies, when using multiple texts, I particularly focus on the question: How do the sources differ and what might contribute to those differences? In the Spanish–Aztec encounter, for example, the sources tell very different stories of what happened. This is frustrating and enlightening for students because it shows that history is not about what we know happened but rather a conversation about our sources, how we know what happened, different points of view, and the meaning of the past. We may look at, or create, corroboration charts for those sources to identify the differences and explain them. Was one author not there? Was there a bias? Did later memories of the events paste themselves on to the author's text?

This debrief strategy ensures that students are getting the "historical thinking" aspect of the class. In recent years, though, I've increased homework turn-in by bringing the readings into the role-play. When students respond to the texts through diary entries, we can then debrief the homework either by having a few students read their homework or we can have a small fishbowl "café conversation" in which four "characters" get into roles to discuss the compelling question while the rest of us observe and then provide feedback and input.

Reading of Background

The background reading for a role-play sets the context for the subsequent scenes. In literature, the background is the immediate one or two pages right before the conflict and choice moment. The author, of course, writes this part for us. The task for the teacher is to make sure students (especially those who have not read) have a basic understanding of the movement of the plot and characters in the previous pages. This means a brief overview of major plot points that tie together the story enough for all students to be able to participate actively, and understand, the subsequent role-play.

To ensure that all students have a grasp of the scene and conflict that serves as the context for the choice moment, I normally ask students to read for homework only until 1–3 pages before the conflict. We then read those final 1–2 pages of background together until we identify the conflict but before the choice/response is made.

In history, we need to write the background. I normally read the short text, slowly and in a somewhat dramatic voice. You may also print out copies and have students read it. A brief excerpt of a background could be something like this:

The regular people on the street, the members of the Third Estate, have other concerns as well. The price of bread has doubled and bread is essential for their diet. Members of the upper class are concerned about defending their property. They organize a militia, called the National Guard, to be filled with "respectable citizens" who will defend their stores and home. Mobs begin marching down streets, pillaging bakers' shops and threatening to burn down theaters.

Comprehension Check of Background

Since the background provides key information for understanding the role-play that follows, I typically end it with a quick comprehension check—at times something as simple as: "What are three main points that help us understand what is taking place?"; "What's the situation or conflict here?"; Or, I use a targeted question, such as "What seems to concern the members of the 3rd Estate?"

Set the Scene

I begin the scene by calling "characters" into the empty center of the room: the stage. We need to actually get the characters and observers in position. For example, in a later scene in *The Pearl*, this means to turn off the lights, get the two "sleeping" trackers to lie down, get the third tracker to sit near them, place Juana in a corner, and Kino about five feet away from them.

Develop the Conflict with Introduction, Speaking Cards, and First Actions (Historical Only)

I read a quick introduction of 2–4 sentences that sets the parameters of a particular conflict or choice and the exact time and place of the scene. For example, in my "Schools and Family" lesson in the Nazi Germany unit, the scene begins with the following: "During the faculty lunch break, three of the teachers are quietly sipping coffee and eating their lunch. They are talking about some of their recent lessons. Suddenly, a few police officers open the door and enter the faculty lunchroom." We transition to the conflict and the choice moment through the use of a speaking card. In this case, I need the officer to create a conflict, so I provide him with the card, which instigates tension, conflict, and a choice moment.

Card 3A (Officer)

"Teachers, Wejish children are no longer allowed in our schools. You must go to your classes and tell the Wej children to go home."

Identifying a Choice Moment: Defining the Stakes and Options

Once we have a conflict, I now present certain characters with a choice moment:

Choice Moment 1 (Teachers)

The police officers have demanded that you expel your Wejish students. What do you do?

This point in the lesson can be quick, but it is crucial. We want to set up the tension here by verbalizing the conflict, the options the character must consider, and the stakes of that decision. For students who are nervous about role-playing, or need some intellectual scaffolding, having the group help define the possible choices and why they are important can allow all to participate. Perhaps the class identifies three choices for the protagonist, but the student in the scene needs to make the ultimate decision.

One issue that the teacher must play with is whether to analyze the choice before or after the student makes it. Find your style. I tend toward giving the students a brief initial try, pausing for a larger reflection and analysis described above, and then redoing or continuing forward with that scene. The most important time for learning is not during the action but in between it. The pause for group analysis and for advice is where the deeper understandings get developed. There is no single recipe for how long to do the role-play and how long to pause. I tend to not actually let a scene go on for more than 3–4 minutes without a pause to recollect.

Role-Play of Choice Moment

This is the period of true action and dialogue in which the students fully interact with each other, speaking as the characters. I normally begin it with "3, 2, 1—Action" and then they go. When this takes place as a second go-round after a pause, it is remarkable how the reflections and advice reorient the scene and how the depth and quality of the interactions improve in the second (or third) go-around. At the end of this chapter, I provide in-depth suggestions and models for managing the action. In Chapter 6, I include transcriptions of actual role-plays that have taken place in my classroom.

Pausing for Analysis

During the pauses, I have a few stand-by questions that I choose from that lead to the richest part of the lesson. What are the options? What can our "therapists" tell us about what is going on in the characters' heads? What suggestions can our life coaches give? Why is this a difficult decision? Why is your character making this choice?

One question to always have in your pocket: "How realistic is the character's choice so far based on her identity and the situation?" This sometimes involves re-establishing that identity by asking a student to read her original character card. When the wife of a prominent rabbi says that she doesn't care about a boycott of Jewish stores, we need to relook at the identity and the stakes to think about the reaction and to help that student through. This doesn't mean that the entire role-play should be about group identity politics, especially if the character descriptions are nuanced, but it does mean taking into account likely reactions given a person's place in the society.

For a literature class, a highly effective move at moments of doubt is to ask all students to refer back to the text for clues for that character. Based on prior descriptions and actions, what is that character most likely to do?

At times, I use the following prompts to help students think through their characters' decisions.

Things to Consider in Making a Decision

1. What is your character's identity? What factors in that identity may influence your choices?

2. What has happened in previous role-plays that could affect your decision? What choices have you or other characters made?
3. What are the possible consequences of your decision?
4. What does your character care about most?

Reaction: Role-Playing Again, Continuing the Scene, or Trying Out More than One Option

Think about revisiting the same scene multiple times to improve the depth of students' choices and reasoning as well as their ability to articulate and vocalize as their characters. Intersperse this with more pauses for reflections and advice. This cycle is extremely valuable. It is fascinating how repeat attempts at the same scene, interrupted by advice and input from the observers, lead to deeper role-plays and more profound understandings of the characters.

Repeat of Steps 6–10 With a New Scene and Choice Moment

If there is more than one scene in the lesson, we move forward with new characters if necessary, a new introduction, more speaking cards, choice moments, action, pauses for reflection, reaction, and debrief.

Final Debrief

The closing debrief is a seed for students to think about what happened and why it was important. It may include many of the same questions as the mid-scene pauses. We focus on the characters' feelings, their sense of guilt or pride in their actions, and/or predictions of where this will take them in the historical story or the piece of literature. They should evaluate their choices and those of their companions. The observation templates include some of my favorite prompts for debrief and/or exit cards.

- One important moment was when . . .
- One thing I wonder . . .
- I agree with the choice to . . .
- I disagree with the choice to . . .

The Action

How do we actually manage the action and acting—the points in which students are truly role-playing? Here, I provide detailed tips on effectively directing the action, whether fighting or dialogue.

Running a Strategic Planning Scene

Let's take a scene from a French Revolution role-play in which students figure out how to storm the Bastille. I've read the background and the characters are in place. Students have their speaking or action cards.

I have one other key ingredient in my hand: a 20-sided die, which you can buy at any gaming store. Real D&D uses multiple dice (including 4- and 6-sided ones) for different types of actions. For me, one all-purpose 20-sided beauty will do.

We use the die to determine the success of many of the choices or actions that students make, unless it involves them convincing another character to do something through conversation. The die adds in some of the true unpredictability of life. The higher the number, the greater the success, but the cut-off number for "victory" varies depending on the situation and the actual chance of succeeding. Here's an example. A French soldier decides to shoot a musket at a member of the 3rd Estate. If he rolls a 7, then he misses (over the left shoulder!). If he shoots a 12, he hits the man in the left calf and the man stumbles. With a 19 or 20, the musket ball could go straight into his throat and the man falls to the ground, dead on impact.

This works the same way for a negotiation or a skill action. Let's say that members of the crowd outside the Bastille want to convince the official to let them into the prison. First, I'd have the student make the actual argument. Then, he or she might roll if the discussion was inconclusive. A higher roll convinces the official (especially if the student's own argument was persuasive), a middle roll (8–12) might continue the conversation, and a lower roll is unsuccessful. In the same vein, a student might try to climb a wall and enter the prison over the roof and the roll of the die determines the level of success.

Table 3.1 is an example of how this might look in the classroom, with a short excerpt of a scene from a French Revolution role-play when those characters of the 3rd Estate are gathered outside of the hated Bastille prison looking for gunpowder to arm their muskets. I've just read a description of the scene that makes it clear that they want to get into the building. We've discussed what is at stake and the characters' options. I've placed a couple of the students who are soldiers on one side. I ask them to arrange the desks to make a fortress. Perhaps they might put a couple of chairs on the desks to mimic ramparts. If I've managed to get a hold of a trebuchet from a physics teacher, then I give it to them.

In the left-hand column I include the script. The right-hand column is how it would unfold in class, with additional comments.

In this scene, the dice make the role-play more enjoyable because of the added tension. One of the students could have rolled a four when jumping across the roof and would have ended up with a broken leg. Lastly, the dice provide the teacher, or game-master, with some more ability to control the events to allow them to be more historically accurate. Imagine, for example, that students who are role-playing Spanish soldiers decide that they want to kill Montezuma. This is a problem for the role-play because it would be a significant event that is historically inaccurate. What do you do as the teacher? One option is to not allow it. Another is to pull the kids aside and tell them it is not the right time but eventually they will do something to Montezuma and they'll have a few ways of doing that. The third option is to use the dice. Put a series of obstacles in front of them and they have to roll high numbers each time to succeed. Probability says that if you can think of enough obstacles, then they won't succeed—although I do admit that there have been times when I tried that and to my chagrin the student rolled a 20 and I had to allow him to succeed!

Running an Intra-Familial Conflict and Negotiation Scene

These types of scenes are often the most intense and memorable of a unit, even more so than the battles. Here, whether in literature or history, we can generally put aside the dice and allow the drama of the dialogue to take over. I provide two fully developed scripts of such scenes in the literature chapter, but let's consider two examples here. In one case, a mother must explain to her children that they are leaving for Great Britain on a child transport without her. In another, from *A View from the Bridge*, the uncle, Eddie, arrives home to find his niece, Catherine, coming out of the bedroom with an undocumented immigrant who is staying in their home named Rodolpho. The tension of this scene is exacerbated because Eddie has unnaturally strong, perhaps incestuous feelings, for his niece and believes that Rodolpho is gay and using her to get papers.

Table 3.1 A Sample Role-Play Script: On Paper and in Action

Description in the Document	Added Spontaneous Dialogue and Action in the Classroom
Crowds are just arriving beneath walls, hundreds of people are there shouting. **Card 3B (Member of 3rd Estate)** "We want the Bastille! Out with the troops!"	*Teacher:* Crowds are just arriving beneath walls, hundreds of people are there shouting. We're going to start the role-play now. Make sure you're in character. And we're going with 3, 2, 1 "action." *Teacher:* Okay, who has card 3B? Shout it out. *Student:* **"We want the Bastille! Out with the troops!"**
Teacher reads: The mob becomes denser and denser. People push forward. Two drawbridges spanning the moat are pulled up. **Choice Moment 3** How will you try to get into the fortress?	*Teacher:* The mob becomes denser and denser. People push forward. Two drawbridges spanning the moat are pulled up. *Teacher:* We have a choice moment here. Members of the 3rd Estate, you want to get into the Bastille but it is closed off. How do you do it? *Student 1 (Chris):* Maybe we can break down the door of the fortress with an axe? *Student 2 (Marcus):* Really, a fortress door? And how are we going to get across the moat?
Teacher reads: A few of you notice the roof of a building next door that is a bit lower than the fortress. From the roof, you could possibly get across to the Bastille. Two men try to climb up on the roof of one of the shops.	*Student 1 (Chris):* Should we swim across? *Teacher:* Let's pause to see if any of our life coaches have any advice. *Observer 1:* Maybe someone has a rope that they can use to get over the building? *Student 3 (Angie):* I have a rope, maybe one or two of us can throw the rope across, climb over, and lower the drawbridge so everyone else can get through. *Teacher:* Great idea. A few of you notice the roof of a building next door that is a bit lower than the fortress. From the roof, you could possible get across to the Bastille. Two men try to climb up on the roof of one of the shops.
	Teacher: Okay, who is going to give it a try? Let's have Angie since it was your idea. Who else? A few students raise their hands. *Teacher:* Sure, Bob and Miguel. Angie, roll the die to see how you do. Angie rolls a 4.

Table 3.1 continued

Description in the Document	Added Spontaneous Dialogue and Action in the Classroom
	Teacher: Angie, you start to climb up and you get terrified. You start to shake and you fall off, spraining your left ankle. Bob?
	Bob rolls a 14.
	Teacher: All right, Bob, you're up on the roof. What do you do?
	Bob: I'll lower the rope for Miguel to come up.
	Teacher: Miguel, give it a roll.
	Miguel rolls a 10.
	Teacher: Well, not that hard to get up a rope. Miguel, you're up too. What do you both do?
	Miguel: Can we jump across to the Bastille?
	Teacher: With a good roll.
	Miguel: What happens if we get a bad roll?
	Teacher: A very long hospital stay.
	Bob: Okay, I'll do it.
	He rolls a 16.
	Teacher: Okay, you're over and you use the rope to get Miguel over too.
Teacher reads: They dash along roof, and jump on other side of moat. They break into guardhouse and grab axes and sledge-hammers. **Choice Moment 4** What do they use them for?	*Teacher:* They dash along roof, and jump on other side of moat. They break into guardhouse and grab axes and sledgehammers. *Teacher:* We have a choice moment. What will you use the axes and sledgehammers for? *Bob:* Let's cut the drawbridge to lower it so everyone else can come in.
Card 3C (Member of 3rd Estate) "*Liberté, egalité, fraternité!*" *Teacher reads:* The members of the mob slash at the pulleys of the drawbridges. There is a rattle of chains, the drawbridges begin to move, and the bridge falls. One man is killed. Suddenly shots are heard. Who started firing? We're not sure.	*Teacher:* The crowd below sees the bridge lower. It only adds to the excitement. Who has Card 3C? Yell it out. *Student:* "Liberté, egalité, fraternité!" *Teacher:* The members of the mob slash at the pulleys of the drawbridges. There is a rattle of chains, the drawbridges begin to move, and the bridge falls. One man is killed. Suddenly shots are heard. Who started firing? We're not sure.

In both scenes, the most important move is to push students beforehand to define the stakes and the options for the characters. By doing this we increase the tension and move them toward more realistic and deeper acting (and thinking). In the historical scene, students begin to point out that the mother sees survival at stake for her children but also their feelings for her. In terms of options, they debate whether she should be truthful to them or try to soften the situation.

Similarly, the pre-action discussion about the scene in *A View from the Bridge* leads students to evaluate the various emotions and goals that are in play: Catherine's desire for independence, Rodolpho's need to pacify Eddie while also impressing Catherine, and Eddie's pride. They consider the options for violence, argument, and reconciliation.

The important point to remember here is that students might not hit the right notes in their first or second tries. The child might unrealistically yell at the mother, Eddie might giggle in nervousness, or Catherine might hit Eddie. This is where the pauses, reflection, and advice come in, and can be used to get students closer to a deep understanding (and acting) of the characters during this moment of conflict, tension, and choice.

Running a Battle Scene

The Aztec–Spanish Encounter role-play includes at least four major battle scenes, each of which has its own dynamic. In these, almost all the students can be involved and the action is fast-paced, at least in our minds.

Let's take a scene after the Spanish massacre of Aztecs during a religious festival. We've established that the Aztecs are furious and want revenge. The Spanish characters have decided to march through the streets to show their strength and courage and the Aztecs have chosen to ambush them. At times, I've actually had students playing Spanish characters step outside and then allowed the Aztecs to hide in various places in the room. When they walk back in, I read that the Aztecs cry out "The strangers have murdered our warriors" and that "Mexican warriors attack the Spanish soldiers with a fierce assault, armed with swords, clubs, slings, darts, and arrows. Most of all, they use their mighty spears."

Here, it is important to know the outcome. In this battle, the Aztecs must win and drive the Spanish back to the palace. To accomplish that, I allow each Aztec to roll two or three dice for their attacks since they greatly outnumber the Spanish and have the advantage of numbers and familiarity with the terrain. Here's a short excerpt of how part of the scene might play out.

Teacher:	Axoquentzin, you'll attack first. Where are you?
Axoquentzin:	*(standing on a chair)* On a roof.
Teacher:	Who do you attack? With what?
Axoquentzin:	I'll shoot my arrow at Martin.
Teacher:	Roll! Since you have surprise and there are so many of you, roll two dice.

Axoquentzin rolls a 17 and a 7.

Teacher:	Okay, the arrow flies from your bow and goes straight into Martin's midsection. Martin, you're badly hurt and fall to the ground, the arrow sticking out. Tlacotzin, what do you do?
Tlacotzin:	I take my club and run toward the Spanish. I'm going after Cortés!
Teacher:	He has armor so you roll only one die.

Tlacotzin rolls a 3.

Teacher:	You rush toward Cortés and trip over the body of a Spanish soldier who has been killed. You fall and sprain your ankle. We're going to give three more Aztecs a shot to attack before the Spanish figure out what to do.
Tzoyectzin:	Let me go! I'm going to take a sword and attack Mase Escasi, the Tlaxcalan!

Teacher gives two dice to Tzoyectzin who rolls an 18 and a 14.

Teacher:	You rush up to Mase Escasi; he tries to defend but your sword slices all the way through his right bicep, cutting off his arm. Mase stays standing, but blood is pouring out.

Turbo-Boost Role-Plays: Following the Characters and Using the Attributes

There is a "turbo" or advanced level of role-playing that adds layers of interest to the unit. A turbo-boost involves keeping track and tracing the growth of the characters over time, including giving them increasing (or decreasing) attributes like dexterity or force based on what they have done or homework they completed. This is particularly valuable in a unit that occurs over a long period (like the Nazi Germany role-play) but it can be done in all of them.

There are a few ways to turbo-boost. One is to keep a chart of each character with his/her basic information (name, job, etc.). Depending on the characters' experiences in a role-play, I then alter their fate prior to the following lesson and announce it at the beginning. For example, in one role-play an officer might fail to control a boycott of stores. Based on that, he might lose his job at the start of the next lesson. At the beginning of each lesson, I announce a few characters who have experienced major life changes. People can get promotions, have children, get married, be cheated on, get sick, lose a loved one, become unemployed, etc.

At times, I have based the "fate" of the character not only on what happened during the role-play but also on a chance roll of the die at the end of class. Students roll to define their well-being in the intervening days or years between scenes. A roll above 15 might lead to a promotion or marriage, while a roll of 4 could mean sickness or unemployment. This just adds such a layer of fun as the students get so nervous to see what will happen to them.

Along with that, I might add a point to a character's strength, dexterity, health, or another attribute if that person made a key choice or was particularly successful in an action. This works particularly well if you have developed the habit of checking characters' attributes before a key action. "Hey, before you discuss this with Montezuma, remind me of your personality score?" "Chris, before you shoot that arrow, what is your dexterity?"

Role-Play Observer Sheet

Name: _____

Title of role-play: _____

Date of event: _____

What are three key pieces of information from the background that help set up our scene?

1. _____

2. _____

3. _____

Your Role Today: Life Coach[1]

Task: You will not be directly involved in the role-playing today but you have a crucial task. Life coaches give suggestions and strategies for helping us get out of difficult problems. Choose two important moments that happen in the role-play. Explain what happened at that moment and what your advice is to that character.

Character: _____

Table 3.2 Life Coach Observations

	What was Happening	Advice
Moment 1		
Moment 2		

Choose three of the sentence stems to finish:

One important moment was when . . .

_____

_____

One thing I wonder is why . . .

_____

_____

I agree with the choice . . .

_____

_____

I disagree with the choice to . . .

_____

_____

Executing the Role-Play Cheat-Sheet

1. Assign characters and handing out character and speaking cards.

2. Read background and comprehension check: the background sets the context for the scene and provides key information for what took place since the last one.

3. Set the scene: call "characters" into the center and place them in position. Make clear exactly where and when the scene is taking place.

4. Develop the conflict with introduction, speaking cards, and first actions: Read 2–4 sentences that outline a particular conflict or choice. Use cards as catalysts for the conflict.

5. Identify a choice moment; define the stakes and options. Make sure the nature of the conflict is clear, the options the characters must weigh, and the stakes of that decision.

6. Role-play of choice moment. Here is when the students fully interact with each other, speaking as the characters. They are on their own.

7. Pause for analysis. Here are some questions to spark discussion and suggestions:

   - What are the stakes at this moment for these characters?
   - What are the characters' options? Which is the best option?
   - What contributions can our observers make to understand this situation?
   - Why is this a difficult decision?
   - Are the characters making healthy and respectful choices?

8. Reaction: role-play again, continue the scene, or try out more than one option. Consider revisiting the same scene multiple times to improve the role-play.

9. Final debrief. Here is when students do the deep reflection. Some useful prompts:

   - What do we learn from this?
   - Did the character make the right choice? Why or why not?
   - What is hard about this for the characters?
   - What was one emotion that you imagine the characters felt? Why?
   - Were the characters' choices realistic? Why or why not?
   - What is one thing you wonder?

Note

1. Other observer sheets, including therapist, artist, and poet are available for download on my website.

2

Examples of Historical Role-Plays

CHAPTER 4 | The Aztec–Spanish Encounter

The role-play gives us an understanding of the people in history. We get to experience their experiences. I think it's a great way to learn. You can't learn as much from a lesson compared to a role-play. Lessons are boring and students don't learn much because of that.

(Nolan, 9th grader)

Figure 4.1 David as Hernán Cortés, Rolling the Dice

Historical Context of the Role-Play

The Aztec–Spanish encounter, within a global history course, fits into a study of the transition to the Early Modern World and the Age of Exploration and Colonization. In my curriculum, this role-play makes up part of a unit about the role of individuals in changing the world, which I call *Heroes and Villains*. We investigate how people in the past, such as Hernán Cortés, Galileo Galilei, and Martin Luther, made choices that shaped our history and our world.

History courses, in an attempt to reach intellectual sophistication, often teach big ideas (like "Guns, Germs, and Steel") at the expense of individuals and the "history-lite" of biographies. But people of the past, and their choices, are often what fascinate us. Most adults who read history lean toward the biography and if we want to prepare students to become lifelong learners of history, the stories of individuals are great places to start. I read some biographies in graduate school. If we can "do" biographies there, why can't we bring the gripping and exciting stories of individuals into our curriculum and embed them within larger historical events and transformations?

My desire to focus on individuals stems not only out of the "interest" factor, but also because our students are, in some sense, people in training. This is the time in their lives when they hold on to remnants of their childhood but also explore what type of adults they want to be. I wanted to develop a course that would help them reflect upon what it means to be an individual in the larger world, what it means to be great, and the importance of our choices. Besides teaching about transformative historical events, the focus on role-playing and the stories of individuals brings out issues of power, the difficulties of being human, the choices people need to make to achieve greatness, and an exploration of the type of people the students want to become.

Hernán Cortés is the axis of the unit and the role-play because the standard narrative places him fully in the "villain" camp. Many argue that he was responsible for the horrific Native American genocide. He was ruthless and his conquest led to the decimation of a brilliant indigenous civilization through war, disease, and colonization.

I want my students to question everything, however. More complexity emerges when we delve into the details of his story. It brings out the question of intentions versus consequences. What exactly did he set out to do and why did his efforts end up the way they did? To what extent was he responsible for the war that took place and the smallpox epidemic? In what ways should we judge him by our values or his? Was he an intolerant religious extremist or was he right to try to end a practice, human sacrifice, that he legitimately believed to be savagery? Can we take into account the Spanish viewpoint from the time, that he was a brilliant conquistador, soldier, and tactician who overcame overwhelming odds to conquer one of the world's great empires, with only perhaps about 1,000 Spanish soldiers at his command? Some might argue that we need to provide the answer for the students. I argue that we provide the story and the sources and help them work through the evaluation.

Cortés's story is compelling and complex, sometimes mysterious, and it lends itself to a thoroughly engaging and thought-provoking role-play and in-depth analysis of competing primary sources. The rich array of complementary and competing primary sources, from both Spanish and Aztec voices, lends a lovely stich to the tapestry of this unit. It is a class they will remember for the dynamic role-play, but they will also develop historical thinking skills like perspective, sourcing, corroboration, and the use of evidence.

The role-play, which is the centerpiece of the unit, has evolved considerably over time. It began with *Broken Spears* as the main source, and students role-played scenes from that text and then read *Broken Spears* for homework. I now include a central Spanish text, *The Discovery and Conquest of Mexico*, as well. The first time I did it with students, there was more direction in what they had to do. Now, I provide more "choice moments" that allow them to move their characters either in the direction described in Diaz del Castillo's work or in *Broken Spears*.

There are a number of historical questions that we can ask and answer when learning about the Spanish–Aztec encounter. I start with an overarching compelling question: How did a very small group of Spanish soldiers manage to conquer one of the most powerful empires in the world? From there, I move on to a number of supporting questions that lead us through the unit and role-play.

- What was Cortés's mission?
- Were the initial encounters between the Spanish and indigenous Americans positive or negative?
- Why did the Spanish, Aztecs, and Tlaxcalan leaders make the choices that they did?
- Who was stronger: The Aztecs or the Spanish?
- Why did the war and conflict begin?
- Why did each side choose to record and remember the history in the way that it did?
- What were the effects of the Spanish conquest?
- Why is the story of this encounter important?

Suggested Reading

Diaz del Castillo, B. (2004). *The Discovery and Conquest of Mexico*. Boston, MA: Da Capo Press.

Bernal Diaz del Castillo was a participant in the Aztec–Spanish encounter, a foot soldier who wanted to set the record straight about the role of common men like himself in this event. He was 23 years old when he arrived in Mexico in 1519. He wrote the text years later, in the 1550s, when he was in his seventies, which he called *The True History of the Conquest of New Spain*. It is considered the "great chronicle" of the Spanish–Aztec encounter.

Leon-Portillo, M. (2006). *Broken Spears: The Aztec Account of the Conquest of Mexico*. Boston, MA: Beacon Press.

Miguel Leon-Portillo edited this book, which has become the go-to account of the Aztec–Spanish encounter from the Aztec perspective. He provides direct translations of Aztec accounts that were written down in the first decades after the encounter. He relies most heavily on Sahagun's *Florentine Codex*. As the editor, Leon-Portillo gives us excerpts of the original text.

Levy, B. (2009). *Conquistador: Hernan Cortes, King Montezuma, and the Last Stand of the Aztecs*. New York: Bantam.

Buddy Levy provides a highly readable and fair account of the Aztec–Spanish encounter. While not a professional historian, he uses a wide array of primary and secondary sources very nicely, and weaves them into a compelling account of the conquest.

Thomas, H. (1995). *Conquest: Cortes, Montezuma, and the Fall of Old Mexico*. New York: Simon & Schuster.

Hugh Thomas is an esteemed historian of the Americas and his book *Conquest* is an excellent academic source on the Spanish–Aztec encounter.

Before the Role-Play

I situate my Aztec–Spanish encounter role-play within a larger context of the Age of Exploration. Prior to beginning the unit, we examine the Middle Ages, feudal roles, Spain in 1492, basic Christian theology surrounding salvation, the medieval Christian hierarchy, and the motivations of explorers. It is also worth considering spending some days looking at pre-Columbian Aztec civilization.

The Scope of the Role-Play

This game begins with events just prior to the meeting between the Spanish and the Aztecs and it ends with the final capitulation of the Aztec king to Hernán Cortés. The main activities take place in the following sequence.

Introduction: Creating Characters

1. The acceptance of Cortés's mission and his escape from Cuba.
2. An Aztec–Tlaxcalan battle and human sacrifice.
3. An Aztec meeting on the coast.
4. Pivotal Decision Debate: Should the Tlaxcalans ally with the Spanish?
5. Cortés and Montezuma meet.
6. The Banquet.
7. Kidnapping of Montezuma.
8. Attack in the Plaza.
9. Pivotal Decision Debate: What should each side do vis-à-vis the other?
10. Return of the Aztecs.
11. Noche Triste.
12. Plague.
13. Surrender.

Assessments

For this role-play, I give two quizzes and students do a benchmark writing task on the question "Was Cortés a hero or a villain?" A second skill-based task is a take-home project about Cortés that asks students to express their understanding of him as an historical figure and his significance, in one of three ways: through a letter collection from the perspective of someone in the encounter, through an artistic memorial (sculpture), or through a traditional essay format.

Full Homework Model

Encounter in the Americas Role-Play

Homework #1

Task: Included are two sources about the Spanish–Aztec encounter. For a higher output grade, add details from these sources into your diary entry. And, imagine that what is in these documents are things that you (your character) have actually seen.

The Basic Assignment: Write 1–2 paragraphs as a diary entry from your character's perspective about today's role-play.

Output Grade	Amount of Output
1.	Do the basic assignment above.
2.	Close-read source A and make references to it in your diary entry.
3.	Close-read sources A and B, and incorporate details from them into your entry. Show how your character responds to sources.
4.	Close-read sources A and B, and incorporate details from them into your entry. Explain fully how your character views the role-play and reacts to the sources including thoughts and emotions, agreements and disagreements.

Compelling Question: What is your view of the Spanish–Tlaxcalan alliance?

Source	Title or Author
A.	*Broken Spears*: pp. 38–9.
B.	Diaz del Castillo, pp. 122–4, 152–6.

The Aztec–Spanish Encounter Intro

Creating a Character

The Gist

We create characters and get excited about the upcoming role-play.

I usually use a number lottery or online random name generator to order the students' picks since no two students can have the same character.

Only allow about 25 per cent of the class to be Spanish characters in order to keep the population ratio somewhat realistic.

I provide the worksheet below for them to fill out once they have their characters and the slip that describes their identities. Students need to choose a name/person, three skills that they think would help that person, and two pieces of equipment. Then, they assign the six number values to the six attributes. I explain that they can only use each number one time. The highest number, 17, becomes their best attribute and if they need to use that to succeed in a task they will have a greater likelihood of doing so.

Once they have done all of that, the students make a name-tag (folded paper) for their character, which they should have with them every day. On the front should be the character's name and job. On the back, all the skills, possessions, and attributes. This will be helpful for everyone during the role-play.

Character Choices

See Tables 4.1, 4.2, and 4.3 on the next two pages.

1. Choose your character.

2. Choose three skills that would be helpful to you based on your character's job.

3. Choose two possessions that your character might need.

Table 4.1 Aztec–Spanish Encounter: The Characters

Spanish Characters	Aztec Characters	Tlaxcalan Characters
Hernán Cortés, conquistador	Montezuma, king	Xicotenga the Elder, king
Pedro de Alvarado, second-in-command	Cuatemoc, king's nephew	Xicotenga the Younger, soldier
Gonzalo Dominguez, horseman	Cuitlahuac, prince	Tecpanecatl, Tlaxcalan captain
Cristoval de Olid, soldier	Cuitlalpitoc, ambassador	Acxoxecatl, Tlaxcalan warrior
Fransisco de Morla, captain	Qualpopoca, Aztec administrator and military commander	Piltecuhtli, Tlaxcalan warrior
Gaspar Ortiz, musician	Teotlalco, queen	Textlipitl, Tlaxcalan warrior
Bartolomé de Olmedo, priest	Tlapalizquixochtzin, queen	Mase Escasi, messenger and warrior
Juan Sedeno, wealthy soldier and merchant	Chimalpopoca, Montezuma's son	Malinche, translator
Alonzo de Avila, a captain and treasurer	Tzilacatzin, Aztec general	
Gonzalo de Sandoval, captain	Tzoyectzin, Aztec general	
Antonio de Villafana, soldier	Cuauhcoatl, Aztec priest	
Martin Lopez, master shipbuilder	Tecohuentzin, Aztec priest	
	Axoquentzin, Aztec warrior	
	Tlacotzin, Aztec warrior	
	Tzihuacpopocatzin, Aztec noble and ambassador	
	Tlilpotonque, midwife	
	Chimalma, Aztec woman	
	Citlalli, Aztec woman, wife of warrior	
	Teyacapan, Aztec woman, court servant	
	Erendira, Aztec woman	
	Cuappiatzin, chief of the house of arrows	
	Quetzalaztatzin, keeper of the chalk	
	Topantemoc, Montezuma's treasurer	
	Atlixcatzin, Aztec nobleman	
	Tecatzin, chief of the armory	

My character is: _____

Table 4.2 Character Skills

Carpentry	First aid	Skiing
Composing	Knowledge of science and history	Stealth
Pottery/sculpture		Sewing
Woodcarving	Theater	Public speaking
Forgery	Picking a lock	Drawing
Climbing	Cooking	Math
Repairing broken items	Card tricks	Memory
Writing	Swimming	Gymnastics
Boxing	Running	Handling animals (horsemanship)
Bargaining	Hiking	
Swordsmanship	Musical instruments	Nature survival
	Singing	Archery
		Learning languages

My three skills are:

1. _____ 2. _____ 3. _____

Table 4.3 Character Possessions

Book of prayers	Saw	A gold ring and necklace
Armor (steel for Spanish; leather for Aztec)	Hammer and nails	Needle and string
	Knife	Saddle
Climbing boots	Winter boots	Cooking knives
Compass, magnetic	Calligraphy set	Large suitcase
Bow and arrows	Paints	2 water bottles
Rope	Paper and ink/quill	Chocolate (Tlaxcalan/Aztec)
Violin	*Macuahuitl* (Aztec/Tlaxcalan)	Eggs (Tlaxcalan/Aztecs)
Helmet	Sling (Aztec/Tlaxcalan)	Feathers (Tlaxcalan/Aztec)
Cards	Spear (Aztec/Tlaxcalan)	Jewels (Tlaxcalan/Aztecs)
First-aid kit	Sword (Aztec or Spanish)	Tortillas (Tlaxcalan/Aztec)
Sword	Musket (Spanish)	
	Crossbow (Spanish)	
	Bow and arrow (Aztec/Tlaxcalan)	

My two possessions are:

1. _____ 2. _____

Final Character Sheet

Character Name _____	Character Job _____
Skills: Copy from previous page 1. _____ 2. _____ 3. _____	**Possessions:** Copy from previous page 1. _____ 2. _____

Race/nationality
(Spanish, Aztec, or Tlaxcalan):   _____

Gender: _____

Languages (Spanish or Nahuatl):   _____

Religion (Catholic or indigenous):   _____

Attributes
Assign the following numbers to the six attributes below: 17, 11, 13, 10, 8, 6 points.

Force	___	Dexterity	___	Perception	___
Health	___	Intelligence	___	Interpersonal	___

Force	= Brute physical strength.
Health	= Physical health and ability to withstand and recover from injury.
Dexterity	= Quickness, skill with hands, agility.
Intelligence	= Smartness.
Perception	= Ability to make good decisions.
Interpersonal	= Strong charisma, ability to convince others to take your point of view.

At this point make a name-tag for your character, which should include all the key information that is above.

Tlaxcalan Characters

Note: Full character descriptions are available online at:
http://davidsherrin.wix.com/davidsherrin

Xicotenga the Elder, king: You are a 61-year-old king of the Tlaxcalan people. The Tlaxcalans are the last remaining nation that has not been conquered by the Aztecs and brought into their tribute system. However, you know that you cannot hold out much longer and in all these wars the Aztecs capture your young men and women to sacrifice to their gods. You are cautious in nature and like to hear various opinions before making a judgment. You have a wife and three sons, one of whom, Xicotenga the Younger, you are grooming to take over from you. Your success mission is to maintain the Tlaxcalans independent of the Aztec empire and to improve Tlaxcala's power in the region.

Xicotenga the Younger, soldier and
     prince
Tecpanecatl, Tlaxcalan captain
Acxoxecatl, Tlaxcalan warrior

Piltecuhtli, Tlaxcalan warrior
Textlipitl, Tlaxcalan warrior
Malinche

Aztec Characters

Montezuma, king: You are the 53-year-old king of the Aztec empire. You are used to people listening to you and respecting you. You believe deeply in the Aztec religion and the noble destiny of the Aztec people. You are tall, strong, and have two wives. You consider yourself to be a thoughtful, careful, and curious ruler who thinks through decisions rather than taking rash action. Your success mission is to secure the safety of the Aztec empire and the safety of your people through any dangers.

Cuatemoc, nobleman
Cuitlahuac, prince
Teotlalco, queen
Tlapalizquixochtzin, queen
Cuitlalpitoc, ambassador
Qualpopoca, Aztec administrator
     and military commander
Chimalpopoca, Montezuma's
     son
Tzilacatzin, Aztec general

Tzoyectzin, Aztec general
Temoctzin, Aztec general
Cuauhcoatl, Aztec priest
Tecohuentzin, Aztec priest
Axoquentzin, Aztec warrior
Tzihuacpopocatzin, Aztec noble
     and ambassador
Tlilpotonque, midwife
Cuappiatzin, chief of the house
     of arrows

Quetzalaztatzin, keeper of the chalk

Topantemoc, Montezuma's treasurer

Tecatzin, chief of the armory

Tlacotzin, Aztec warrior

Chimalma, Aztec woman, wife of Topantemoc

Citlalli, Aztec woman, wife of the warrior Axoquentzin

Teyacapan, Aztec woman, court servant

Erendira, Aztec woman, wife of Tzilacatzin and court cook

Spanish Characters

Hernán Cortés, conquistador: You are the 34-year-old leader of an expedition to colonize parts of Mexico in the name of King Charles V of Spain. You come from a poor family of lower nobility status and you have dreams of increasing your rank, fame, and wealth. You understand that you are undergoing a venture in which two previous expeditions have failed when they got into battles with powerful natives. You are embarking with about 300 men under your command and you understand that their lives are in your hand. You have a deep Christian faith and believe that it is your duty to convert the natives to Christianity. Your success mission is to colonize powerful parts of Mexico by making them loyal (or vassals) to your king, to gain great wealth, to convert souls, to gain fame and glory, and to maintain the safety and health of your crew.

Pedro de Alvarado, second-in-command

Gonzalo Dominguez, horseman

Cristoval de Olid, soldier

Fransisco de Morla, captain

Gaspar Ortiz, musician

Bartolomé de Olmedo, priest

Juan Sedeno, wealthy soldier and merchant

Alonzo de Avila, captain and treasurer

Gonzalo de Sandoval, captain

Antonio de Villafana, soldier

Martin Lopez, master shipbuilder

The Aztec–Spanish Encounter 1: The Mission

The Gist: This lesson helps students to understand Cortés's mission. By the end, the characters should have escaped from Velazquez's attempt to stop them and the students should understand why explorers went on this mission.

Homework #1: The Mission

Compelling Question: How did Cortés and his men escape from Governor Velazquez's attempt to stop them?

Source	Title or Author
A.	Thomas, pp. 140–1.
B.	Diaz del Castillo, pp. 32–6.

Warm-up
What would be exciting (or scary) about exploring a new place?

Scenery and Props
- A few plastic swords.
- Some clothes for Cortés: A cape or tuxedo jacket, a brimmed hat with a feather or two taped on, some plastic jewelry.

The Date
February 8, 1519.

Teacher Does
I set the scene by showing images of a white sandy beach. I play background sounds of the waves lapping against the shore or of birds singing. As I begin the narrative of the role-play I cycle through a few images of Hernán Cortés, Diego Velazquez, and caravel ships when appropriate.

Background

Teacher Reads

You are no longer in America. You are no longer in the twenty first-century and you no longer have the names you were born with. It is now February 8, 1519. Your names are Hernán Cortés, Montezuma, Guatemoc, Fransisco, Martin, Citlalli, and more. Those of you who are Spaniards are on the beach of Cuba. Europeans have been in Cuba for almost thirty years now, ever since Columbus's first voyages. You are on a white, sandy beach surrounded by other Spanish explorers and Taino Indians. Many of the Tainos have become slaves to the Spanish under the *encomienda* system. Many others have died from disease.

The day is hot, the sun burns on your skin. You've taken a dip in the water but now you lounge on the sand under a palm tree. You've traveled so far on your caravel ships, across an ocean, farther than almost anyone in history. Your loved ones, your wives and children and parents, are on the other side of the sea. This is the Age of Exploration. You and your peers have set off on search for spices, gold, adventure, souls, and fame.

Scene 1: The Mission

Teacher Reads

A man stands before you, a nobleman who has stood out from the others. He wears a velvet cloak trimmed with gold. Indian slaves follow him. He has been an assistant to the Governor, Diego Velazquez. He wants to convince you to follow him from the island to the mainland, where he has heard there is a wealthy civilization with riches beyond anything you can imagine. He declares to you all:

Card 1A (Cortés)

Action: Stand up in front of the Spanish soldiers.

"Comrades, let us follow the sign of the holy cross with true faith, and through it we shall conquer. These are the orders that I have received from our honorable governor, Diego Velazquez: 'The purpose is to serve God. We may not sleep with native women. We must treat the natives well and tell them of the power of our king. We will declare that they are under the rule of Charles V and take possession of the place, to populate, and to discover.'"

Teacher Does
Directs the student with Card 1B to stand and read.

Card 1B (Any Spanish Soldier)

"Why should we go?"

Choice Moment 1 (Cortés)

You must provide convincing reasons why they should go with you. What will you say?

Teacher Says
Who wishes to join Cortés on his expedition? Walk over to him.

Choice Moment 2 (Spanish characters)

Cortés wants to know if you want to join his expedition. What do you do?

Teacher Reads
You are gathered at the beach. The majestic caravels, beautiful ships, are ready to take you off the island toward this wonderful civilization. About 350 men are gathered who have followed Cortés. Unfortunately, the Spanish governor, Diego Velazquez, has become fearful of Cortés's growing power. A messenger arrives.

Card 1C (Messenger NPC[1])

Governor Velazquez has sent me to say that he is recalling you. You must return to the capital and forget about this expedition.

Choice Moment 3 (Spanish characters)

Governor Velazquez wants you to turn back. What do you do?

Teacher Tip

Students normally choose one of two options. Either they try to convince the messenger to join them and go aboard the ship or they attempt to kill him, steal anything he has, and hide the body. Give a few attempts, have them roll dice to gauge their success, but in either one they should be successful. The historical record (as seen in the homework) differs on what actually took place, thereby opening avenues for creativity.

Discussion Moment

I usually pause here and ask the students what they thought about Cortés's choice. Was it the smart decision? Was it the right thing to do? At this point, students start to name some other options, including bribing the messenger, taking him captive, ignoring him, etc.

Teacher Tip

This past year I tried something new. After that discussion, I said: "Hey, let's role-play an alternative scenario." So they brainstormed a few possible options that the Spanish could have taken. We tried again, but this time they had to convince the messenger to join up rather than kill him.

Aztec–Spanish Encounter 2: Human Sacrifice

The Gist: Today we ramp up the emotion of the role-play with a re-enactment of an Aztec–Tlaxcalan war and the resulting ritual of human sacrifice. Students end up with an understanding of why the Tlaxcalans will develop an alliance with the Spanish.

Homework #2: Aztec Human Sacrifice

Compelling Question: What is your view (as your character) of Aztec human sacrifice?

Figure 4.2 Students Role-Playing Aztec Human Sacrifice

Source	Title or Author
A.	Glancey, J. "The Templo Mayor: A place for human sacrifices." BBC. www.bbc.com/culture/story/20150227-a-place-for-human-sacrifices[2]
B.	"Aztec Massacre." PBS. www.pbs.org/wnet/secrets/aztec-massacre-program-transcript/97/[3]

Warm-up

Option 1: So far, do you think Hernán Cortés is a hero or a villain? Why?

Option 2: Do you think it is ever okay to hurt someone in the name of religion? Why or why not?

Scenery and Props

- A drum, masks, fake blood, fake heart sword/knife, crown for Montezuma.

The Date
February 8, 1519.

Background

Teacher Reads
Those of you who are Aztecs are gathered in the main plaza of Tenochtitlan. It is an imposing sight to see the majestic pyramids rise before you. You see the great leader himself, Emperor Montezuma II, stand before you in front of his palace. He is filled with a sense of apprehension and fear. A series of evil omens have foretold of disasters to come. Over the last few weeks you have all seen a fiery comet cross the sky. All of a sudden, the great temple of Huitzilopochtli, the god of war, burst into flames. The lake that surrounds you, the Lake of Mexico, boiled and rose above the banks, flooding into houses. Montezuma begins a speech.

Scene 1: The Aztec Mission

Card 2A (Montezuma)

"The gods are angry. We need to go to war to appease them. Our warriors shall go against the Tlaxcalans. They are the one nation that has not submitted to the mighty Aztecs. Bring me back prisoners! Warriors, rise up!"

Choice Moment 1 (Aztec warriors)

Aztec warriors, who will follow Montezuma's command?

Teacher Does
Make sure that Aztec warriors stand up and march in a line around the room. Give them any props you might have like plastic swords.

Teacher Reads
The Aztec warriors march toward the Tlaxcalan tribe armed for war with spears, clubs, slings, bow arrow, darts, and more. It is early morning, just before the

sunrise. Many are also protected with thick cotton armor and armed with the *Macuahitl*, a wooden club that has obsidian stone on its edges. The Tlaxcalan characters are getting water for the day, waking up their children, and eating breakfast.

Scene 2: The Battle

Key reminders: Make sure that each Aztec student knows what weapon he or she is using. Give them the chance to attack first because of surprise. Each Aztec character should choose a Tlaxcalan to attack. They roll the dice and anything above a 12 should be a hit. Anything above a 16 is a serious hit. A 19 or above should be fatal or near fatal. Allow the battle to go on for 5–10 minutes. Try to allow some "damage" or injuries to take place but it is still early for any characters to die.

Choice Moment 2 (Aztec Warriors)

You have some Tlaxcalans who are injured on the battlefield. What would you like to do with them?

Scene 3: The Sacrifice

Teacher Reads
The battle is short. The goal is not to kill the Tlaxcalans. Instead, the Aztecs take Tlaxcalans prisoners and carry them back to Tenochtitlan. (*Choose two Tlaxcalan characters.*) The brother of _____ and the uncle of _____ have been taken captive. The Aztec warriors cross the bridge leading into their capital and soon thousands are gathered at the main plaza. They drag the fearful prisoners toward the giant pyramid, their main temple. At the top are five high priests of the Aztec religion.

Card 2B (Warrior)

"We demand that you give this prisoner as a gift to our gods. Take his blood and feed it to our lord!"

Teacher Directs

One student becomes an NPC (the Tlaxcalan prisoner) and lies on a desk with a few Aztec characters in a circle around him or her. A student beats on the drum.

Teacher Tip

We actually have models of the human anatomy in the science room that allow me to take out a few organs to have ready. If not, it is fine to print out pictures of a heart or a liver. Have the priest "do" everything that you read.

Teacher Reads

The prisoner is dragged to the top of the pyramid. The crowd watches in awe. The priest slowly takes an obsidian knife and slices into the Tlaxcalan's mid-section. With experience and skill, he rips out a still beating heart. He holds it high in the air and the crowd chants. The prisoner dies as he sees his heart held above him.

Card 2C (Priest)

"This gift of human blood is for our god, the sun. May you rise each day!"

Teacher Reads

Prisoner after prisoner is brought to the pyramid and sacrificed to appease and feed the Aztec god of the sun. By the end of the ceremony, blood is pouring down the steps of the pyramid to the ground below.

Wrap-up and Debrief

Why did the Aztecs not try to kill the Tlaxcalans in war? What was the purpose of this war? Were the Aztecs wrong to sacrifice these prisoners? How do you think the Tlaxcalans will feel about the Aztecs and their leaders?

Aztec–Spanish Encounter 3:
The Ambassadors

The Gist: We delve further into our analysis of Hernán Cortés's actions and the difficulties of cross-cultural encounters as he and the Spanish meet Aztec ambassadors for the first time.

Homework #3: The Ambassadors

Compelling Question: You will have a debate tomorrow about a possible Spanish–Tlaxcalan alliance. How does your character feel about that possibility? Write a one-page proposal about how you stand. If you want an alliance, what can you offer the other side and why should they join with you?

Source	Title or Author
A.	Leon de Portillo, pp. 25–9.
B.	Diaz del Castillo, pp. 69–73.

See Figures 4.3a and 4.3b overleaf.

Warm-up
Option 1: What do you think might be some difficulties when messengers from two civilizations meet for the first time?

Option 2: Review questions.

Scenery and Props
I make sure to prepare by readying a number of trinkets for the students to exchange as gifts, whether beads, fashion jewelry, feathers, images of Aztec art. Give these to Aztec ambassadors.

The Date
March 15, 1519.

Teacher Does
During the warm-up, gather the Spanish characters and ask them how they would respond when the Aztec ambassadors arrive: respect and deference or a show of power? Students can choose either approach. If they want to

Keliza's ambassador's homework: Note how she uses her prior knowledge of the Aztec–Tlaxcalan relationship to provide incentives for the Tlaxcalans to join an alliance with the Spanish soldiers.

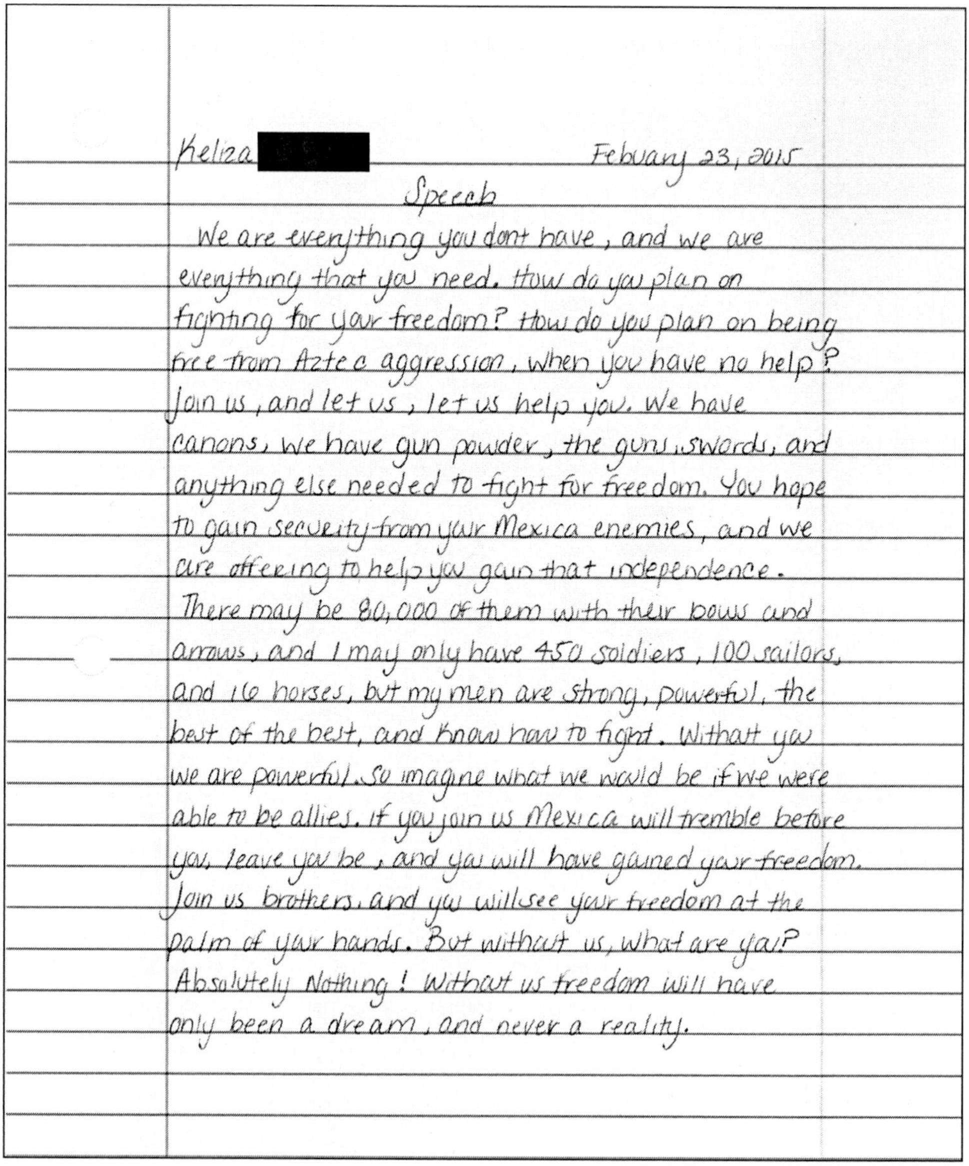

Keliza ▓▓▓   Febuary 23, 2015
                    Speech
   We are everything you dont have , and we are
everything that you need. How do you plan on
fighting for your freedom? How do you plan on being
free from Aztec aggression , when you have no help?
Join us , and let us , let us help you. We have
canons, we have gun powder , the guns, swords, and
anything else needed to fight for freedom. You hope
to gain security from your Mexica enemies, and we
are offering to help you gain that independence.
There may be 80,000 of them with their bows and
arrows, and I may only have 450 soldiers , 100 sailors,
and 16 horses, but my men are strong, powerful, the
best of the best, and know how to fight. Without you
we are powerful. So imagine what we would be if we were
able to be allies. If you join us Mexica will tremble before
you, leave you be , and you will have gained your freedom.
Join us brothers, and you will see your freedom at the
palm of your hands. But without us, what are you?
Absolutely Nothing! Without us freedom will have
only been a dream, and never a reality.

Figure 4.3a Keliza's Speech for Aztec–Spanish PDD

Shania's ambassador's homework: Taking the other side, Shania capitalizes on the fear of the unknown in her attempt to convince the Tlaxcalans not to ally with the Spanish.

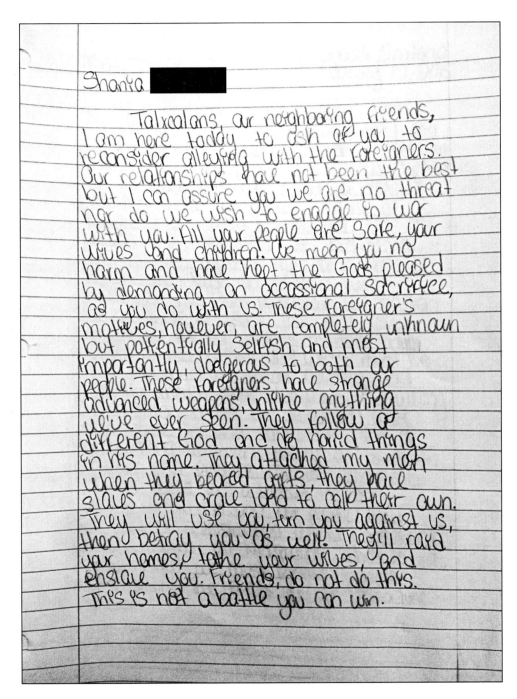

Shania

Talxcalans, our neighboring friends, I am here today to ask of you to reconsider allewing with the foreigners. Our relationships have not been the best but I can assure you we are no threat nor do we wish to engage in war with you. All your people are safe, your wives and children. We mean you no harm and have kept the Gods pleased by demanding an occassional sacrifice, as you do with us. These foreigner's motives, however, are completely unknown but potfentially selfish and most importantly, dangerous to both our people. These foreigners have strange advanced weapons, unlike anything we've ever seen. They follow a different God and do horrid things in his name. They attacked my men when they beared gifts, they take slaves and crave land to call their own. They will use you, turn you against us, then betray you as well. They'll raid your homes, take your wives, and enslave you. Friends, do not do this. This is not a battle you can win.

Figure 4.3b Shania's Speech for Aztec–Spanish PDD

demonstrate power, ask how they will show their power to intimidate the Aztec messengers. Without fail, after a few ideas a student thinks of using the guns and horses. During the role-play, when Cortés says "Go" they will shoot their guns in the air and yell "bang" and then some riders on horses will gallop around.

Background

Teacher Reads

After the Spanish arrived on the coast of Mexico some of the men still loyal to the Governor of Cuba conspired to seize a ship and escape to Cuba, but Cortés moved swiftly to quash their plans. To make sure such a mutiny did not happen again, he sank his ships to prevent anyone's return. He also hung the leader, cut off the feet of another, and gave a third 200 lashes.

They almost immediately get into battles with smaller Mexican tribes that live by the water. Using their guns, steel armor, and horses, the few Spanish troops are able to defeat much larger armies with very few losses. The Spanish receive gifts from this tribe, including some of the Tabascan women. One of them is named Malinche. The Spanish baptize her and call her Dona Marina. She speaks many of the local languages and quickly learns Spanish. She becomes Cortés's interpreter.

In Tenochtitlan, Montezuma receives messages about these powerful foreigners who speak another language and have come from across the waters. This is happening in the year I-Reed in the Aztec calendar, the exact year that a legend and prophecy foretold that the god Quetzocoatl would return to the shores of Mexico.

Montezuma decides to send his best ambassadors, the leader being a man named Tendile, and spies to the coast to meet with the strangers to learn about them, to bring gifts, and to scout them out.

Teacher Tip

Aztec students with gifts should stand and line-up. Cortés, any noblemen, and 2–3 soldiers should stand and face the Aztecs.

Scene 1: The Meeting

Teacher Reads (and Students Mimic)

The Aztec ambassadors arrive on the coast. The head ambassador, Tendile, is gorgeously dressed in a parrot-feather cloak. Montezuma had instructed his steward to supply and feed his guests. He, and then the other Aztecs behind him, walk up to Cortés, put a finger to the earth and then raise it to their lips. He lights incense, carefully slices a knife across his arm, bleeds himself, and then offers his blood on straws.

Card 3A (Montezuma's ambassador)

Action: Put your finger to earth in front of Cortés and kiss your finger.

Card 3B (Cortés)

"I am the ambassador of the king who rules the greater part of the world. Send my best wishes to your king, Montezuma."

Card 3C (Cortés)

"I would like to meet your prince so we can trade."

Card 3D (Tendile)

"Please accept now this present which we give you in his name."

Teacher Reads (and Students Mimic)

The Aztec messengers appear one after another giving gifts to Cortés, valuable objects like plums, chickens, turquoise masks, headdresses with feathers, decorated vests with disk of gold, feathered shoes with gold, and more.

Choice Moment 1 (Cortés)

You have two options. Do you: A) Greet them warmly and thank them with a smile and give them glass beads in return; or B) Do you say: "Is this all? Is this your gift of welcome? Is this how you greet people?"

Scene 2: On the Beach

Teacher Reads

The Spanish invite the Aztecs to gather round on the beach. The Spanish decide to give them a show.

Teacher Tip

Give the sign, a "go," for students to "shoot" their guns in the air or gallop around on horses.

Choice Moment 2 (Aztec Ambassadors)

What will you say to Montezuma about the strangers when you return to Tenochtitlan?

Wrap-up and Debrief

How did this role-play go from the Spanish perspective? What about from the Aztec perspective? What do you think the Aztecs would say to Montezuma about the strangers when they return? How do you think the Aztecs felt about the Spanish behavior? Why did Cortés make his choice in how to respond to the Aztec gifts?

Teacher Tip

After the debrief, consider role-playing an alternative scenario. Go back to Cortés's choice moment. How did he respond? What other options did he have? Allow them to role-play an alternative response and evaluate how the Aztec feelings change based on the new interaction. Which response do they think was more likely to happen? Interestingly, both options are accurate depending on the source used.

Aztec–Spanish Encounter 4:
Pivotal Discussion Debate on Spanish–Tlaxcalan Alliance

The Gist: The role-play helps bring out a key moment of the story, which is when the Spanish and Tlaxcalans make an alliance. Through the PDDs, students must clarify their characters' position regarding this possible alliance and its implications for them and their group.

Homework #4: The Alliance

Compelling Question: What is your view of the Spanish–Tlaxcalan alliance?

Source	Title or Author
A.	Leon de Portillo, pp. 38–9.
B.	Diaz del Castillo, pp. 122–4, 152–6.

Warm-up
Prepare for the PDD (see format below).

PDD 1
The Alliance Meeting.

The Date
March 30, 1519.

Background

Teacher Reads
On the coast, the Spanish make an alliance with a small nation called the Totonacs that had been conquered by the Aztecs and forced to pay tribute to Montezuma in food and slaves. The Totonacs provide some soldiers and guides for the Spanish and some women. Cortés insists that the Totonacs remove their idols from their temples. They refuse, and he holds their chief hostage at swordpoint. Cortés's men climb to the top of the temple and throw the idols to the ground below, shattering them in pieces. He burns the pieces, cleans the temple of blood, and then places a cross at the top.

The Tlaxcalan chiefs, Xicotenga and Chichimecatecle, hear that the Spanish are coming toward them. Cortés sends messengers to them asking for peace and a meeting to discuss an alliance. They know that the Spanish have met with Aztec ambassadors. The Tlaxcalans are the only tribe that has not been conquered by the Aztecs. The chiefs call a Council of Elders to discuss the situation. The Aztecs, hearing that the Spanish are attempting an alliance with the Tlaxcalans, also send three ambassadors to make their position known.

The Spanish enter the city of Tlaxcala and all the Indians are on the roofs and in the streets, thrilled and eager to see the strange foreigners. They shower them with native roses and give them comfortable beds to sleep on. The Spanish soldiers are in amazement at the spacious and well-built palaces, the intricate stonework, the orchards and gardens, the variety of trees, roses, and flowers. They enter the main palace for their meeting.

Card 4A (Xicotenga and Chichimecatecle)

Ladies and gentlemen, my brothers and sisters, my fellow Tlaxcalans. Strange men from across the waters have arrived in our world. They are here with us now. My understanding is that they have a proposal to make for us for an alliance. We have also received visitors from the Aztecs. While we are often at war with you, we welcome you to this counsel of peace. I have my own advisors here as well. This is a confusing time for all of us. We need to hear your view and then we, the Council of Elders, will make a decision for the Tlaxcalans.

Format of PDD

1. Tlaxcalan welcome (Card 4A).
2. Spanish leaders read proposals.
3. Aztec ambassadors read proposals.
4. Tlaxcalan advisors read proposals.
5. Open discussion and debate.
6. Decision (by vote) of the Council.

Teacher Tip

This is the only scene that is slightly ahistorical in that there were no Spanish ambassadors, to my knowledge, at the meeting. However, getting all students involved in this PDD is important. In Diaz del Castillo's text, the Spanish and Tlaxcalans first fight, and the Spanish win, before an alliance is struck. This is one time when we need to push the story in the right direction. By the end, some type of loose alliance between the Spanish and Tlaxcalans has been formed.

PDD 2
In Montezuma's Palace.

The Date
April 3, 1519.

Background

Teacher Reads
The Spanish arrival in Mexico has created a firestorm of anxiety among the indigenous nations. Despite the small number of foreigners, with their powerful weapons they have defeated any army that has tried to stop them. To many, it appears that they have the spirit of Quetzocoatl behind them. The Spanish have now created a loose alliance with the Tlaxcalans and Cortés and his men are marching toward Tenochtitlan atop their mighty beasts.

After leaving Tlaxcala with a small group of Tlaxcalan warriors, Cortés and the Spanish marched to Cholula, a town 20 miles from Tlaxcala. While in the city, the Tlaxcalans warned Malinche, Cortés's trusted confidante, interpreter, and now lover, that the Cholulans were planning to trap Cortés inside the city and massacre his army. When the Cholulan leadership and many of their warriors gathered, unarmed, in a great enclosure by their pyramid temple of Quetzalcoatl, the Spanish and the Tlaxcalans killed them. It was a brutal massacre of unarmed civilians. The news of the massacre, of Cortés's boldness and ruthlessness, and of his ability to defeat the Tlaxcalans, quickly reached Tenochtitlan. It had a chilling effect.

Cortés has sent a message that he wishes to meet with the great Montezuma to tell him of his wonderful king Charles V, to discuss ways they might work together, and to expand the peaceful alliances he is bringing to the region. He says he wants to be a partner with the great Montezuma.

Format of PDD

1. Montezuma's welcome (Card 4B).
2. Aztec advisors make arguments about what to do.
3. Open discussion and debate.
4. Decision by Montezuma.

Card 4B (Montezuma)

Ladies and gentlemen, my brothers and sisters, my fellow Aztecs. Strange men from across the waters have arrived in our world. They are coming towards us. They look different. They speak different. They have weapons of fire. They have defeated all who come against them. They say they want peace with us and that they want to become like brothers. My advisors, what should we do?

Aztec–Spanish Encounter 5: Cortés and Montezuma Meet

The Gist: Today we try to delve deeply into the minds of our characters and into their motivations. The event is the first meeting between Cortés and Montezuma.

Homework #5: The Leaders Meet

Compelling Question: How do you view the meeting that took place between Cortés and Montezuma? What would you like to see happen between them next?

Source	Title or Author
A.	Leon de Portillo, pp. 63–4.
B.	Diaz del Castillo, pp. 192–6.

Warm-up
Why did the Spanish and Tlaxcalans ally with each other? What did each want to get from the other?

Scene 1: Meeting of the Leaders

The Date
November 8, 1519.

Scenery and Props
Jewelry, a broom, and some flowers.

Background

Teacher Reads
Cortés and his men march toward the Aztec capital. They are about 400 soldiers in total, wearing their finest armor and battle regalia and accompanied by a small group of Tlaxcalan guides. When they reach Tenochtitlan they are stunned. Mountains and a lake surround the lovely city. Four causeways, or

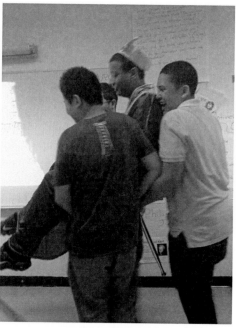

Figure 4.4 Aztecs Giving Gifts to Cortés

Figure 4.5 Students Carrying Montezuma

bridges, lead into the center city, each with drawbridges that the Aztecs could raise or lower. To Cortés the city is as large as the grandest in Spain.

They arrive at the gates of the city and must wait. Montezuma is coming. They see him arriving from the distance. A group of men carry him above their shoulders in a litter. He is wearing a majestic robe with gold sandals. His servants sweep the ground before him as his litter moves forward.

Teacher Tip

Have Montezuma sit in a chair. Get a few of the strongest students to lift him in the chair. Carry him toward Cortés with another student sweeping the floor in front of Montezuma as he moves forward, aloft.

Teacher Reads

Montezuma is about 40 years old, tall, thin but muscular. He has rather short hair and kind eyes. He steps from his litter.

Card 5A (Montezuma)

Action: Place a necklace of gold and precious stones around Cortés's neck.

Card 5B (Montezuma's Men)

Action: Bring your finest flowers, gold, necklaces and give them to Cortés, showering him with presents. Put flowers and necklaces around his necks.

Card 5C (Cortés)

Action: Place a necklace of pearls and cut glass around the neck of Montezuma.

Card 5D (Montezuma)

"You are weary, our lord. Now you have arrived in our city and can rest. You have come to govern the great city of Mexico . . . to descend upon your seat, which for a moment I have guarded for you."

Card 5E (Cortés)

We are your friends, there is nothing to fear. We love you well and our hearts are contented. We have come to your house as friends. There is nothing to fear.

Choice Moment 1 (Cortés)

Montezuma is welcoming you into his city. Do you enter Tenochtitlan with him?

Wrap-up and Debrief

How was this interaction between Cortés and a native leader similar or different from previous ones? What did Montezuma mean by "You have come to govern the great city of Mexico?"

Aztec–Spanish Encounter 6:
The Banquet

The Gist: This lesson develops a tangible "feeling" for the concept of the "Columbian Exchange," to show the initial positive interactions between the Spanish and Aztecs, and to show how actions related to religion (religious intolerance) served to widen the gulf between the two civilizations.

Homework #6: The Banquet

Compelling Question: How is the interaction between the Spanish and Tlaxcalans going from your perspective? What advice do you have for the leaders?

Source	Title or Author
A.	None.
B.	Diaz del Castillo, pp. 204–10.

Warm-up
Should we judge people more by their goals/desires or their actions? Should we judge people by what they do for their community/country or for humanity?

The Date
November 9, 1519.

Scenery and Props
Necklace, hot chocolate, rice, corn chips, sugar, salsa, coffee, and pita. Set up the desks in one long "banquet" table, cover with a tablecloth, and make sure to have paper plates, cups, napkins, etc. ready. I heat up the hot chocolate ahead of time and prepare all the food in plates on a side table.

Background

Teacher Reads
The Spanish soldiers enter Tenochtitlan, walking down a straight and wide causeway that is crowded with Aztec onlookers. The Aztecs gathered round are shocked by the horses that carry some of the Spanish men. The lake

becomes crowded with canoes. Aztec citizens throw flowers to welcome the Spanish and gather on the roofs of houses to gape at and watch the strange visitors.

The Spanish are in awe of the most majestic city they have ever seen. More than 60,000 natives come to one of the center markets to buy and sell gold and silver, lead, brass, copper, tin, stones, shells, bones, and feathers. The Aztecs lead the Spaniards into the heart of the city where Montezuma showers them with more gifts and then quarters them in lavish apartments in the palace where his father had ruled and lived.

Card 6A (Montezuma)

You and your brethren are in your own house, rest awhile. Then come join me at my palace for dinner. I want to treat you as honored guests.

Scene 1: The Banquet

Teacher reads

The Spanish arrive at Montezuma's palace for dinner. Servants bring out about thirty dishes: turkey, pheasant, quail, duck, deer, boar, pigeons, rabbits. Montezuma sits on a low stool, drinking from a gold chalice. He gives Cortés a rich necklace made of golden crabs, which he puts around Cortés's neck.

Card 6B (Montezuma)

Action: Stand and put a necklace around Cortés's neck.

Teacher Tip

We move into a ritual exchange of gifts, our Columbian exchange. The student reads the card, finds the right gift, and then distributes it. After each person presents a gift, we pause for a few moments to eat or drink.

Card 6C (Aztec)

We present to you, our lord, this gift of our sacred *Chocoatl* or Chocolate. It is a tasty drink, especially mixed with peppers. It is wonderful for your health.

Card 6D (Spanish Soldier)

We give to you, our lord, this gift of healthy grain. We call it rice, or *arroz*. You boil it to soften and then it adds strength to your diet.

Card 6E (Aztec)

This gift, Lord Cortés, is of corn. Many of our greatest foods are made of this grain. Bring it back to your land and use it well.

Teacher Tip

I pause for a moment for a dance show. Ahead of time, I've downloaded a couple of videos of traditional Aztec dance. I show a minute or two of the videos as if Aztec dancers have entered the banquet.

Card 6F (Spanish Soldier)

"This present, Lord Montezuma, is to sweeten your world. It is sugar, or *azúcar*. You have never tasted anything like it. It comes from the gods and will add delight to every meal."

Card 6G (Aztec)

"I am honored to give you, Hernán Cortés, a food made of the tomato. It is red like the blood of the earth and will make your veins flow with energy."

Card 6H (Spanish Soldier)

"Our last gifts to exchange with you, Lord Montezuma, are coffee and wheat, café and trigo. The coffee, when brewed correctly, will give you energy in when you are most weary. The wheat can be formed into almost anything—cakes, breads, and more. You will enjoy them both.

Teacher Tip

Second dance show!

Scene 2: The Request

Teacher Reads

During a pause in the dinner, Cortés turns to Montezuma and says something that he has said to all of the native leaders he has encountered.

Card 6I (Cortés)

We worship one true God and your gods are devils and evil. We need to put up crosses and want to build a church. I want you to stop your human sacrifices. Stop your false worship."

Choice Moment 1

Montezuma: Do you: A) Accept Cortés's demand and end the practice of human sacrifice; B) Say: "We have worshiped our gods from the beginning of time and know them to be good. No doubt yours are good too, but do not tell us any more about them."

Teacher Tip

This is a great moment to pause for advice from observers.

Wrap-up and Debrief

How would you describe the atmosphere at the banquet? What changed the atmosphere? How does your character feel about Cortés's request of Montezuma? How do you view Montezuma's response?

Aztec–Spanish Encounter 7:
The Kidnapping

The Gist: The role-play helps us understand why the Spanish kidnapped Montezuma and how that altered the political balance of power in Tenochtitlan.

Homework #7: The Kidnapping

Compelling Question: How did the Spanish treatment of Montezuma influence your character's view of the situation in Tenochtitlan?

Source	Title or Author
A.	Leon de Portillo, pp. 65–9.
B.	Diaz del Castillo, pp. 226–31.

Warm-up
If you saw someone do something you thought was wrong in the name of religion should you try to stop them? Was Cortes right or wrong to try to stop the Aztecs from practicing human sacrifice?

The Date
November 19, 1519.

Scenery and Props
Tortillas, eggs, chicken, wood, pottery, and gold.

Teacher Does
During the warm-up, gather the Spanish team together. Explain that the Aztecs are annoyed at their presence. Things are getting tense in the city. You have about 400 men and there are about 150,000 Aztec warriors in the city. They can raise the drawbridges and trap you at any time. What do you do?

Students normally brainstorm a few options. Sometimes a student comes up with the idea of kidnapping Montezuma. If necessary, ask them what they could use or take to gain power over the Aztecs. Every year, kidnapping Montezuma comes up soon. They need to come up with a plan to do it.

Teacher Tip ✔

This year, students came up with four different plans: (1) to pretend to apologize to Montezuma and to invite him to the palace to teach the Spanish about Aztec religion; (2) to seduce Montezuma with women; (3) to offer to teach Montezuma about Spanish weapons and technology if he comes over to their palace; (4) to invite Montezuma to a banquet at their palace.

Teacher Reads

In the days following their arrival, Cortés and his men marvel at the treasures of Tenochtitlán, the wealth of the market, the beautiful animal skins, and the strange foods like snakes and moles. They are horrified by the Aztec religious rites of human sacrifice. They are particularly amazed by the *chinampas*, the man-made floating gardens in the lake that the Aztecs use to plant crops. The Spanish witness the native sport, *tlatchtli*, which used a rubber ball and had deep religious meaning.

Figure 4.6 Students Conspiring to Kidnap Montezuma

Cortés and Montezuma spend a lot of time together. Montezuma takes him around the city to show him Aztec culture. One day, they climb together to the top of the Great Pyramid and Cortés seees the central altar. He says that he can't imagine how such a great prince like Montezuma could worship false idols, which are actually the devil. Montezuma tells him to speak no more of these religious matters.

Cortés has received word from the coast of a terrible incident. One of Montezuma's officers, at a town on the coast, ambushed and killed six Spanish soldiers. It is unclear whether this attack was ordered by Montezuma or if the officer and his men did so on their own.

Teacher Does

Allow the Spanish team to launch into their plan to (successfully) kidnap Montezuma. I prefer to have the students role-play their own scene but if necessary the cards below can be used. I enjoy watching the student playing Montezuma react as he/she begins to realize what is happening. I saw one student just slump down and sit into a chair as she realized that she wouldn't be able to leave the Spanish "palace." I like to stop at a few points and ask Montezuma to describe his/her feelings at each moment: anger, confusion, betrayal, etc.

Card 7A (Cortés)

"I have no desire to start a war or to destroy this city. Everything will be forgiven if you now come quietly with us to our quarters, and make no protest. If you cry out, you will immediately be killed by these captains of mine."

Card 7B (Montezuma)

"I cannot be made a prisoner. Even if I should agree, my people would not. Take instead my son and two daughters."

Scene 2: The Prisoner

Teacher Reads

Montezuma is now a prisoner in the Spanish palace and the atmosphere in the city has changed. Officially, he still rules and makes the decisions but he often needs to consult Cortés.

Teacher Tip

You might want to consider removing the Spanish group to a corner to secretly debate "Choice Moment 1" (below). If needed there are cards below to move students in the direction of using Montezuma as a hostage to get food and wealth from the Aztecs. It is too early if the Aztecs decide they want to kill Montezuma. It is not possible to do all of these scenes in one class period so it is up to you to pick which you think will be most relevant and helpful.

Choice Moment 1

Montezuma is now your prisoner. What do you want to get from the Aztecs? How?

Card 7C (Spanish Soldier)

"Let us fire some cannons to scare the Aztecs and show our power."

Option 1: Asking for Food

Card 7D (Spanish Soldier)

"Now that we have Montezuma, we can use him to get things from the Aztecs. Let's have him get tortillas, eggs, chicken, wood, and pottery from his people. Montezuma, speak to your people and get those things."

Card 7E (Montezuma)

Action: Stand up and convince your people to bring food and other goods to the Spanish.

Choice Moment 2

Aztecs: Who brings food to the Spanish?

Option 2: Asking for Gold

Card 7F (Spanish Soldier)

"Montezuma, bring us to your treasure room. We want gold."

Card 7G (Montezuma)

"I will bring you to the treasure house, but it is locked. How will we get in?"

Teacher Tip ✔

This is a fun moment for the Spanish team to try to break into the treasure room before some Aztecs see them and soldiers arrive. I give them a few tries to use their "dexterity" to break in. Hopefully, they'll figure out who has the best chance to do so. We roll some dice as the Aztecs approach to see if they can steal the treasure.

Teacher Reads (If the Spanish Succeed)

They spend three days in the treasure room. There is so much gold in jewelry and statues that the Spanish think they have found El Dorado: fine bracelets, necklaces with large stones, ankle rings with gold bells, royal crowns, royal finery, gold bars. They melt all the valuable items into gold bars, giving 2 percent to the king, 20 percent to Cortés; the rest to the soldiers.

Option 3: Trying to End Sacrifice

Teacher reads

Hernán Cortés has gained near total control of the city of Tenochtitlan. However, the practice that he reviles, human sacrifice, continues. He marches to the top of the Great Temple with soldiers and pushes the priests aside. Montezuma hears of this and rushes to the Temple to meet Cortés. Aztecs gather below.

Choice Moment 3 (Montezuma)

Do you: A) Allow Cortés to destroy the idols? B) Beg Cortés to stop and offer to allow him to build a cross on the temple so they can share the space?

Aztec–Spanish Encounter 8:
Attack in the Plaza

The Gist: Why did the Spanish attack/massacre the Aztecs in the plaza and how did this change the dynamics in Tenochtitlan?

Homework #8: The Attack in the Plaza

Compelling Question: How did the attack in the plaza influence your view of the current situation in Tenochtitlan? Write a speech/proposal about what you think your group should do next.

Source	Title or Author
A.	Leon de Portillo, pp. 72–5.
B.	Diaz del Castillo, pp. 296–8.

Warm-up
How do you think the kidnapping of Montezuma will change life in Tenochtitlan?

The Date
May 5, 1520.

Background

Teacher Reads
While Cortés rules Tenochtitlan along with Montezuma, an unexpected event takes place on the coast. Diego Velazquez, the Spanish governor of Mexico, has sent an armada of soldiers and horses to confront Cortés and to retake control of the mission. It is a terrible challenge to Cortés's authority after he has done so much to establish Spanish power in Tenochtitlan. Cortés knows that he cannot allow all that he has struggled for to go to someone else.

Card 8A (Cortés)

I am going to stop this Spanish invasion with some soldiers. Pedro de Alvarado, I am leaving Tenochtitlan under your control. I am leaving you 150 men.

Teacher Reads

After Cortés leaves, the atmosphere in Tenochtitlan immediately changes and becomes tenser. The Aztecs, who had been so cooperative with Cortés there, suddenly stop bringing food to the Spanish soldiers. Montezuma becomes withdrawn and rarely communicates. Pedro de Alvarado begins to receive reports of strange behavior among the Aztecs.

The festival of Toxcatl, one of the great religious holidays for the Aztecs, is approaching. Alvarado allows the Aztecs to celebrate the festival but insists there should be no human sacrifice. Days later, walking around the town he sees long stakes in the ground, perhaps to hang victims. Women are seen preparing the statues.

Card 8B (Tlaxcalan)

Señor Alvarado, we have heard that after the ceremony the Aztec warriors will attack you.

Choice Moment 1 (Alvarado)

Do you: A) Do nothing? B) Take three leading Aztecs and torture them with burning sticks against their stomachs until they talk?

Teacher Tip

If Alvarado chooses to torture, the Aztec reveals that they are going to revolt and attack the Spanish.

Scene 1: The Festival

Teacher Reads

The Aztecs gather in a plaza to celebrate their gods Huichilobos and Tezcatepuca. It is a wonderful party with their finest ceremonial costumes, quetzal feathers, fine animal skins, and jade jewelry. There is drumming, flute playing, and dancing.

Teacher Tip

Play some Aztec (or indigenous) music or show a video of Aztec traditional dance, which you can find on YouTube. I make the Aztecs get up and "dance" around the room. Usually the best I can get is a "cha-cha" line.

Choice Moment 2 (Alvarado)

Do you: A) Do nothing and wait for the Aztecs to do something; B) Take a pre-emptive attack and hit them before they can get you?

Teacher Tip

If Alvarado does not choose "B," have another soldier make that choice so that the attack will happen.

Teacher Reads

The Spanish soldiers close in, wearing full battle armor, against the unarmed Aztec priests and noblemen. Musketeers, with guns, are posted along the wall and guards along the gates. The Spanish close the doors to the plaza as the unaware Aztecs continue to celebrate. Alvarado yells out:

Card 8C (Alvarado)

"Let them die."

Teacher Reads
The Spanish move in for a vicious attack with guns and swords.

Teacher Tip

Allow the Spanish soldiers the first attack in the battle. They choose a victim and their weapon. They have a greater chance of hitting because of surprise. Afterwards, ask the Aztecs what their options are. Perhaps they think of fighting back (unarmed), running, or playing dead. They make that choice and roll for success, but their roll has to be higher than normal. Allow the battle to continue for 10–15 minutes. Some characters may die in this scene.

Teacher Reads
The Spanish rush in and use their swords to cut off arms and heads, stabbing them, spearing them, striking with swords, beheading them, and splitting their heads in pieces. They slash their swords across their stomachs and intestines spill out. The blood gathers into pools up to their ankles or knees.

Aztec–Spanish Encounter 9:
PDD on Communal Choices after the Massacre

The Gist: This PDD allows students to explore the political implications after the Spanish massacre of Aztec celebrants. There will be two PDDs: one for the Spanish/Tlaxcalans and one for the Aztecs. If possible, separate them into two different groups so they don't hear each other. If not, they should "pretend" they don't.

Warm-up
Was Cortés responsible for the massacre of the Aztecs?

The Date
June 24, 1520.

PDD 1
The Aztecs.

Teacher Reads
The Spanish soldiers have just massacred your unarmed priests and warriors during a religious festival. They spoke of peace, but your people are dead. Your illustrious leader, Montezuma, is captive in their palace. You have rarely seen him or heard from him.

PDD Debate (Aztecs)

What do you do next?

1. Opening welcome from Cuatemoc, cousin of Montezuma.

2. Characters present their speeches/proposals.

3. Open debate.

4. Aztec noblemen make a decision.

Teacher Tip

The likelihood is that the Aztec team will want to fight back. Allow them to, since the Aztecs did. They may also consider replacing Montezuma with a new ruler and anointing him king. The Aztecs did this also. In this case, the new ruler must be a member of the royal family.

PDD 2
The Spanish/Tlaxcalans.

Teacher Reads
While Cortés was gone, Spanish soldiers massacred unarmed Aztec priests and warriors during a religious festival. You have only a few hundred men in the city. They have millions, including trained warriors. Hernán Cortés has returned from the coast where he has quashed the rebellion of Spanish soldiers and convinced more to join him in Tenochtitlan. He returns to a city that is quiet, empty, a ghost town. No one ventures outside. The Spanish soldiers are all in the palace, unable to leave.

PDD Debate (Spanish/Tlaxcalans)

What do you do next?

1. Opening statement from Hernán Cortés.

2. Characters present their speeches/proposals.

3. Open debate.

4. Decision from Hernán Cortés.

Aztec–Spanish Encounter 10: Return of the Aztecs

The Gist: This role-play highlights the strength of the Aztec military force and their resistance, thereby challenging the traditional narrative of "strong" Europeans and "weak" natives. It also depicts Montezuma's death.

Homework #9: Return of the Aztecs

Compelling Question: How did the Aztec revenge attack influence your view of the situation in Tenochtitlan? What should your group do next?

Source	Title or Author
A.	Leon de Portillo, pp. 76–9.
B.	Diaz del Castillo, pp. 306–11.

Warm-up
Agree or disagree: The massacre of the Aztecs during their religious festival shows that Cortés was a villain.

The Date
June 24, 1520.

Scene 1: The Battle

Scenery and Props
Mock weapons.

Teacher Tip

This role-play assumes that the Aztecs want to fight back, which has never failed to take place in my experience. You should frame the setting of the battle based on decisions they made the previous day. The Aztecs need to win this battle decisively and to drive the Spanish back to the palace. One way to do that is to allow each Aztec character to roll 2–3 dice at a time due to their greater numbers.

Teacher Reads

News of the Spanish massacre of the Aztecs during their religious festival spreads throughout the city. The Aztecs are in an uproar. "The strangers have murdered our warriors," they cry out.

> ## Card 10A (Aztec)
>
> "Bring your spear and shields! The strangers have murdered our warriors!"

Teacher Reads

Mexican warriors attack the Spanish soldiers with a fierce assault, armed with swords, clubs, slings, darts, and arrows. Most of all, they use their mighty spears. It is brutal hand-to-hand combat. The Aztecs pull up the drawbridges trapping the Spanish in the city. The Spanish shoot their guns at the seemingly endless onslaught of Aztecs.

> ## Teacher Tip
>
> Role-play the battle with dice, allowing students to take turns attacking.

> ## Card 10B (Aztec)
>
> I will sacrifice you to my dogs.

> ## Card 10C (Aztec)
>
> I will rip out your hearts.

> ## Card 10D (Aztec)
>
> I will feast on your legs.

Card 10E (Aztec)

I will throw your bodies to panthers and snakes.

Scene 2: The Palace

Teacher Reads

The Spanish are trapped in the palace. They cannot get out. The Aztecs have even started trying to set fire to the timbers that support the building.

Choice Moment 1 (Cortés)

What can you try to use to get the Aztecs to stop?

Teacher Tip

Students will likely consider trying to get Montezuma to stop them. If not, suggest it. He needs to go up to the roof. If he doesn't agree, they can force him.

Card 10F (Cortés)

Montezuma, you need to go on the roof of the palace and speak to your people. Convince them to stop.

Choice Moment 2 (Montezuma)

What do you do? What do you say?

Teacher Reads

Montezuma goes on to the roof and speaks to his people, to the throngs of Aztecs below.

Choice Moment 3 (Aztecs)

What do you do?

Teacher Tip

At least one Aztec will be furious enough with Montezuma to try to kill him. Allow them to shoot arrows or throw stones. Montezuma does die from this encounter, hit by at least three stones in his head.

Teacher Reads

The Aztecs revolt against Montezuma. They launch stones, rocks, and darts toward him. He is hit in the head with stones, falls, and dies.

Spanish–Aztec Encounter 11:
La Noche Triste

The Gist: This lesson is meant to highlight a key moment in the Spanish–Aztec encounter, which is when the Spanish fled the city of Tenochtitlan. We try to answer a few key questions through the role-play: (1) Why did the Spanish try to escape Tenochtitlan?; (2) What does this tell us about the strengths of the competing forces? This lessons serves to break down the traditional narrative of the "strong" European and the "weak" native.

Homework #10: Noche Triste

Compelling Question: How did the "Noche Triste" battle influence your view of the situation in Tenochtitlan? What should your group do next?

Source	Title or Author
A.	Leon de Portillo, pp. 84–97.
B.	Diaz del Castillo, pp. 312–17.

Warm-up
Was Montezuma a hero or a villain?

The Date
July 5, 1520.

Teacher Does
During the warm-up, gather the Spanish students together. Evaluate the situation. The Aztecs are surrounding them and basically have them bunkered down in their quarters. Every time they try to fight back the Aztec forces, far superior in numbers, overwhelm them. What do they want to do? This is essentially a group choice moment, hopefully based on the decision they made in the PDD. Most likely, they want to choose to flee. If not, perhaps hint that they have a few days before the Aztecs launch an all-out assault on their quarters. Once they decide to escape, ask whether they want to do it during the day or at night. Naturally, night is a better choice.

Teacher Tip

I also quickly pull the Aztecs out of the room for them to make their plan, knowing they have the Spanish bunkered down in the palace. Clearly, the Aztecs want to attack. While they are outside the room, I give the Spanish and Tlaxcalan students two minutes to make a bridge across the room. I turn off the lights and they get to work with the desks, lining them up.

Scene 1: The Escape

Teacher Reads
It is late at night, about midnight. The sky is overcast and a gentle rain is falling. The only sounds are those of birds, crickets, and rain, until the group of Spanish soldiers leave their quarters, trying to be as quiet as they can. They arrive on one of the bridges.

Teacher Tip

Use an audio site like soundjay.com to play the sound of rain coming down. I ask the Spanish students to stand up and to gather on one side of the room and then to walk as quietly as they can to the other side atop the desk "bridge."

Teacher Reads
The escaping Spanish soldiers see a Mexican woman drawing water from the canal. If she looks up she will see them.

Choice Moment 1 (Spanish soldiers)

What do you do? A) Try to escape as fast as you can? B) Try to kill the woman before she can make a sound?

Teacher Tip

I give them the chance but arrange it for the woman, or someone else, to see them and shout a warning.

Card 11A (Aztec Woman)

"Cut them off so that not one of them may be alive" "They are crossing the canal! Our enemies are escaping!"

Choice Moment 2 (Aztecs)

What do you do when you hear the call?

Teacher Reads

Hundreds of warriors bear down on the Spanish, on canoes, crossing bridges and charging at them. Each Aztec needs to decide whether you want to attack in a canoe or on the bridge.

Teacher Tip

At this point, those Aztecs in "canoes" need to sit on their chairs and "paddle" them into position. Other Aztecs can get onto the desks to be on the "bridge." Each Aztec now represents 2–3 soldiers. They get to attack first and to roll a few dice. They choose whom to attack. Allow the battle to go on for 5–10 minutes. The Spanish need to decide whether to flee out of the city, to fight back, or something else. Have some Spanish soldiers get killed, fall in the water, get badly injured, or get captured. The Aztecs win, but some Spanish escape, including Cortés.

Teacher Reads
Some Spanish soldiers make it to the other side of the bridge. Mexican warriors leap into boats, trapping the Spanish on either side. It is a storm of arrows, so many are dead, choking the water with corpses.

Choice Moment 3 (Aztecs)

You have some Spanish prisoners. What do you want to do with them? A) Let them go? B) Kill them right away? C) Sacrifice them at the temple to your gods?

Scene 2: Outside the City

Card 11B (Spanish Soldier)

We don't have enough warriors, where can we get more soldiers?

Teacher Reads
The Spanish decide to return to Tlaxcala to rest and recuperate. Hernán Cortés spends days in a coma, unconscious, from his wounds. When he awakens, he and his captains decide to ask Tlaxcalans for 10,000 more warriors.

Choice Moment 4 (Spanish Leaders)

You need to convince the Tlaxcalans to provide more soldiers for another attack. How do you do it?

Choice Moment 5 (Tlaxcalan Leaders)

What do you do? Do you join the Spanish for another attack or do you refuse them? What are the consequences of either choice?

Spanish–Aztec Encounter 12:
The Plague

The Gist: This lesson helps us determine why the Spanish were victorious by outlining the importance of the smallpox epidemic in changing the dynamics of the war. The homework helps us understand difficulties each side faced during "half-time" (after the Spanish had left Tenochtitlan) and then the brutalities, fear, and "war crimes" that took place during the final few months of battle.

Homework #11: Smallpox

Compelling Question: How did the smallpox epidemic influence your view of the situation in Tenochtitlan? What should your group do next?

Source	Title or Author
A.	Leon de Portillo, pp. 92–9.
B.	Diaz del Castillo, pp. 388–90, 415.

The Date
December 20, 1520.

Scenery and Props
I print out pictures of people suffering from smallpox.

The Background

Teacher Reads
Tenochtitlan will never look the same again. It is not just because of the battles that have destroyed its homes, plazas, and temples. It is because of an invisible killer, one the Aztecs cannot understand, that is far more deadly than the Spanish sword or gun. It is smallpox and the plague burns through the city for 70 days. The Aztecs have no resistance to it. It is new to their environment. Sores erupt on their faces, on their chests, on their bellies. So many have died that there are not enough people left to search for food and everyone is too sick to care for them.

Teacher Does

Have the Aztecs roll the die. They need a 15 or higher to escape the plague, but even a 15 or a 16 could mean that they are sick and suffering. Most of them should die. Give them a picture of someone with smallpox to represent that sickness.

Choice Moment 1 (Aztec)

You have the sense that your husband/wife may be infected with smallpox. What do you do?

Choice Moment 2 (Aztec)

You have the sense that your child may be infected with smallpox. What do you do?

Choice Moment 3 (Aztec)

You have the sense that your neighbor may be infected with smallpox. He comes to your home for help. What do you do?

Scene 2: Water

Teacher Reads

The Spanish lay siege on the Aztecs. They surround the city to cut off any access to food or water. The blockade causes starvation. Aztecs are eating lilies and seeds, and chewing on animal skins to survive. The Aztecs' former allies have now seen the balance of power shift. They now line up on the Spanish side.

Choice Moment 4 (Spanish)

The Aztecs still have access to fresh water coming from an aqueduct that they had built. What do you do?

Teacher Tip

If the Spanish try to destroy the aqueduct, have them roll the die to see if they are successful. Either the way, the Aztecs are starving. Now have the Aztecs roll the die again to see how they fare against the starvation. Perhaps they need a roll of 13 or higher to survive. You could consider a choice moment to explore how a family might deal with a limited supply of water.

Choice Moment 5 (Aztecs)

Do you surrender or do you continue to fight? If the latter, what do you do to defend the city?

Scene 3: Battle (Optional)

Teacher Reads

For 93 days, the Spanish try to get into the city. They fight, but, even with a force decimated by smallpox and starvation, the Aztecs repel them. Eventually the disease and hunger is too much. The Spanish advance across the bridges. They bring cannons and go to the top of the pyramid. They see two priests there. They throw them over the side.

Seeing the Spanish at the Great Temple infuriates the Aztecs. They give one last attack and the air becomes dark from the arrows. The Spanish withdraw, but they try again and again, each day. Aztecs cut off the heads of Spanish prisoners and throw them at the Spanish, threatening them.

Choice Moment 6 (Cortés)

Do you offer surrender to the Aztecs?

Choice Moment 7 (Cuatemoc)

If Cortés offers, do you accept surrender or do you try to escape?

Teacher Tip

If Cuatemoc tries to escape, have him roll the dice. Have the students place him in a canoe. He needs an 18 or higher to escape capture.

Choice Moment 8 (Spanish Soldiers)

When you find Cuatemoc, what do you do with him? What do you want him to help you find? What do you do if he refuses?

Choice Moment 9 (Cuatemoc)

You have been found by the Spanish. What do you ask for?

Teacher Reads

The Spanish soldiers, under Cortés's orders, torture Cuatemoc to get information about any hidden treasure. As a result, he limps for the rest of his life.

After the Role-Play

Homework #12: After the Surrender

Compelling Questions: See below.

Source	Title or Author
A.	Leon de Portillo, pp. 116–21.
B.	Diaz del Castillo, pp. 449–54.

The Aztec–Spanish role-play ends with the conquest of Tenochtitlan and the surrender of the Aztec leader. Afterwards, we need to come back to our original questions.

- What was Cortés's mission?

- Were the initial encounters between the Spanish and indigenous Americans positive or negative?

- Why did the Spanish, Aztecs, and Tlaxcalan leaders make the choices that they did?

- Who was stronger: The Aztecs or the Spanish?

- Why did the war and conflict begin?

- Why did each side choose to record and remember the history in the way that it did?

- What were the effects of the Spanish conquest?

- Why is the story of this encounter important?

This is also the time to tie the role-play to a larger context and to other events with which we may be able to make valuable comparisons and contrasts. For the first two days after the role-play we look at primary sources that reveal immediate and long-term effects of the encounter on the Americas, ranging from the introduction of a new language and religion to the importation of African slaves, the creation of a largely mestizo population, the creation of new cities, colonial trade and mercantilism, wars between European powers over colonial territories, and the demographic catastrophe for Native Americans.

Of course, you will want to spend some time after the role-play doing whichever assessments you choose, whether a quiz, in-class writing, or take-home project.

It is also very worthwhile to spend one or two days looking at the Spanish conquest of Peru by Francisco Pizarro. Pizarro learned from Cortés's experience, so it is interesting to see how he adopted and adapted Cortés's methods. This allows us to make valuable connections and to fit the Aztec–Spanish encounter into a larger context.

Notes

1. Ask another student playing an Aztec or Tlaxcalan role to take on this temporary role for today, which we call an NPC, or a Non-Player Character.
2. I suggest that you take out the section that refers to Hernan Cortés to avoid a preview of what is to come.
3. Also take out section about Cortés.

CHAPTER 5

Weimar and Nazi Germany

I enjoyed role-playing to learn about history. It helped me understand how the Nazi Party came to power. It's a lot more helpful than being told what happens, it puts you there.

(Shona, 10th grader)

Role-play has helped me understand Germans. On a first glance that looks terrible but it helps me realize why one of the cruelest totalitarian government came to power with the support of almost the entire population.

(Oliver, 10th grader)

Historical Context of the Role-Play

This unit runs through the period just after World War I and into the start of World War II.

In my class, I include it in a unit called "Genocide and Justice" that involves the Holocaust, Armenian Genocide, and Rwanda. We focus on the "before" and "after" of genocide—the causes, effects, and attempts to achieve post-genocidal justice.

The origins of this role-play stem from my years teaching at the Facing History School, where we implemented the *Holocaust and Human Behavior* curriculum. The focus of our work was on the choices that regular individuals made, the causes of the genocide, and the attempts to obtain justice in the aftermath. I began to search for ways to bring the difficult choices to life, to bring people into the story, and to feel these stories. Consequently, I created my first role-play.

The Genocide and Justice unit is about understanding genocide and about bringing students into a conversation about humanity, moral decisions, and the difficult dilemmas people face during times of crisis. It is about figuring out why groups discriminate against others, the seemingly unlimited capacity of humans to commit brutality, and also the wondrous acts of heroism and altruism that take place in the most dangerous circumstances.

Just like the Aztec–Spanish role-play, the concept of power is central to our study. In what ways do individuals and groups attempt to exert power over others? How can a government take away a group's power? Why do they do that? Perhaps the most important question is whether individuals have the power to dissent, rebel, and resist in the midst of genocidal regimes.

At certain moments, I've wondered if there is a lack of sensitivity to the memory of the victims and survivors by pretending to be in their shoes, especially since we can never truly experience what they did. Over time, I've become convinced that no attempt at history, even the most academic and scholarly tome, can replicate the past and the experiences of individuals in that situation. Because we cannot truly grasp the experience (thankfully) does not mean we should not try to approximate some aspects of it. We only begin to build empathy if we make some attempt to put ourselves there, even if we just barely get off the starting block. My maternal grandparents, who I knew deeply, were both Holocaust survivors and I do think they would be thrilled to know that teenagers were learning about the Holocaust in this way.

This past year I began to do the role-play as a loosely veiled allegory in which the names of the people and places are acronyms for the actual historical persons and locations. The table below outlines some of the most commonly used acronyms. I did this partly because by 9th grade many students have studied the Holocaust and that knowledge of where the events are going surely influences their actions during the role-play. An allegory also frees them up to make truer decisions as their characters without worrying as much about saying or doing something that could be viewed as anti-Semitic. A few of the students will figure out after a day or two the nature of the allegory.

I've made a number of changes to the role-play over the years. Originally, I began with one lesson on the outbreak of World War I and another on the experience of soldiers and civilians during that war in order to build some context. Now I delve right into Weimar Germany at the end of the Great War. A few years ago I began to flesh out the character descriptions and added in some particularly interesting twists, such as the spy, the radical, and the two secret homosexual characters. Depending on the students who take them on, these elements could lead to some fantastic drama. I've switched around the order of a few of the lessons, added in scenes based on student request (such as the "Choices" lesson), and brought the diary entries and Pivotal Discussion Debates into the mix.

Table 5.1 Weimar Allegory Terms

Real-Life	Role-Play
Germany	Nergmay
Berlin	Lerbin
Germans	Nergmans
Jews	Wejs
Christians	Tiaschrins
Nazis	Sizan
Hitler	Terhil

Before the Role-Play

I fluctuate on the idea of what to do before beginning this unit. Most years, I grounded it in a background on the concept of genocide, student inquiry on genocide, and in the context Germany found itself in at the start of the 1920s. It took about five or six days to do that work before jumping into the role-play. This approach gives students the framework to understand what they will be experiencing.

This year, however, we plunged straight into the role-play without any context whatsoever. My thought is that students build deeper inquiry around a concept like genocide after having seen one example of it. Rather than develop questions and a working definition of genocide before studying it, we did so after seeing the first example (the Holocaust) but before encountering other ones like Armenia and Rwanda. By doing so, their questions are richer and they develop a working definition that we can hold to a stricter standard during our further study.

The Scope of the Role-Play

1. History of Anti-Semitism: Medieval era.
2. Choosing a Character.
3. Weimar Republic: Labor Strikes and Unemployment.
4. Weimar Republic: Hyperinflation.
5. Weimar Republic: Great Depression.
6. Pivotal Decision Debate: Who should lead Nergmay?

7. Nazi Party in power: The book burnings and boycotts.
8. Nazi Party in power: The effects on schools and families.
9. Nazi Party in power: The Hitler Youth.
10. Pivotal Decision Debate: What is our future? What choices should we make?
11. *Kristallnacht.*
12. Making our choices and actions.
13. Deportation.

Homework: Reading and Writing

Almost all the suggested homework readings can be found on the fabulous "German History in Documents and Images (GHDI)" website. Each homework assignment includes four sources for students to close-read, which match up with the topic of that day. Normally, two of those are images and two are page-length texts. Each lesson identifies those four sources for you (plus, at times, an extension reading).

On p. 122 I provide a template that I use to assign homework to the students. The task requires them to read the four sources and to write a diary entry from their characters' perspectives answering the compelling question of that day. Given the wide array of student motivation and skill-levels, I give them a range of options to complete. In other words, I make it clear that they can simply write a one-paragraph diary entry based entirely on the role-play (in which case they get a "1"). On the other end, a fully fleshed-out entry that includes details from the four sources as well as thoughtful responses from the character to those texts or images gets them a "4." The only assignments that vary a bit from these are those prior to the Pivotal discussion debates. In those cases, students should write a proposal, instead of a diary entry. I include detailed instructions for those in the relevant lessons.

The spectrum of primary sources that they encounter allows for them to have a broader understanding of the Holocaust and another entrance point into the content. Seeing the source from the character's perspective also helps them build a lens for analysis.

Homework Debrief

I utilize the "café conversation" format for debriefing the homework, especially since it fits so nicely into the "cafe culture" of Europe. Either I choose four students or they volunteer, each of whom sits in the middle of the room. They form a circle. The first few times they read their diary entries to serve as models for other students. We pay particular attention to creative ways in which students can integrate the sources into their entries. One might write: "I was walking down street and I saw a young women holding a sign asking for a job" or "I was looking at the newspaper and I saw a photograph of soldiers saluting Hitler" or "I stopped by my friend's house and was dismayed to see that the parents and four children were sharing a sausage for dinner." All of these would be ways to integrate a photograph fluidly into the diary entries.

Assessments

There are a number of ways that I assess students during this unit. The first is to periodically utilize the role-playing rubric. I also include two quizzes: one quick comprehension quiz on basic vocabulary and a second lengthier one that includes comprehension, perspective, connections, and sourcing. I give them a benchmark essay: "Why did the Nazi Party gain power in Germany?" Depending on the year and the students in the group, I then choose between one or more projects, or give them some choice: (1) a portfolio of their best diary entries with an introduction or conclusion; (2) a sculpture memorial; (3) A letter about "What should be done?" during a particular ethical dilemma; or (4) the Julius Streicher mock trial.

Suggested Reading

Browning, C.R. (1998). *Ordinary Men: Reserve Police Battalion 101 and the Final Solution in Poland.* New York: Harper Perennial.

This book is Robert Browning's exploration of the unique experience of Police Battalion 101, in which the commanding officer gave his soldiers the option to not participate in the slaughter of Jewish civilians.

Facing History and Ourselves. (1994). *Holocaust and Human Behavior.* Brookline, MA: Facing History and Ourselves.

Facing History and Ourselves' principle resource book has background readings and primary sources on the Weimar Republic, individual choices, and attempts at justice.

Fritzsche, P. (2009). *Life and Death in the Third Reich*. Cambridge: Belknap Press.

Peter Fritzsche's secondary source is a strong scholarly look at Nazi Germany. It provides background context for much of the scenarios of the role-play in accessible language.

Goldhagen, D.J. (1997). *Hitler's Willing Executioners: Ordinary Germans and the Holocaust*. New York: Vintage.

Daniel Jonah Goldhagen's scholarly book was controversial when published for his claim that the root cause of the Holocaust was German anti-Semitism. He also argues that there were fewer severe consequences for disobedience or protest under Nazi rule than normally imagined.

Hoss, R. (1996). *Death Dealer: The Memoirs of the SS Kommandant at Auschwitz*. Boston, MA: Da Capo Press.

Rudoph Hoss's memoir is fascinating for how it shows the readiness with which Nazi leaders admitted to what they had done. As a text for studying sourcing, it demonstrates both Hoss's attempts at self-justification and his inability to escape his own anti-Semitism.

Larson, E. (2012). *In the Garden of Beasts: Love, Terror, and an American Family in Hitler's Berlin*. New York: Crown.

Eric Larson's historical narrative provides a riveting view of Berlin in the early years of Nazi rule. It helps establish the climate of fear that rapidly developed under Hitler.

Weissmann Klein, G. (1995). *All But My Life: A Memoir*. New York: Hill and Wang.

This is one of the best Holocaust memoirs I've read, with gripping depictions of deportation, death marches, and liberation. The surprise ending is unforgettable.

Weitz, E.D. (2013). *Weimar Germany: Promise and Tragedy*. Princeton, NJ: Princeton University Press.

This book is a useful secondary source for understanding the tumultuous decade of Weimar Germany. It highlights both the economic difficulties and the exciting cultural transformations.

Zeller, F. (1989). *When Time Ran Out: Coming of Age in the Third Reich.* Sag Harbor, NY: The Permanent Press.

This book is an accessible high school level memoir about a Jewish child in Nazi Berlin, which hits most of the same events that we experience in the role-play.

Suggested Reading (Online)

German History in Documents and Images (GHDI). http://germanhistorydocs. ghi-dc.org/

This website is a go-to source for primary sources, especially letters and photographs, from the Weimar Republic and Nazi Germany. Each source includes a concise background description, which helps with contextualization. This is my essential stop for creating homework assignments.

United States Holocaust Memorial Museum. www.ushmm.org

This website is user-friendly and provides concise background readings for nearly every topic imaginable within Holocaust education. It is particularly helpful to clear up quick points of doubt about dates or historical facts.

Yad Vashem. www.yadvashem.org

The website of the Israeli Holocaust Museum has an especially helpful section on upstanders, or "Righteous among the Nations."

Model Template of a Homework Assignment

Germany between the Wars: Unemployment and Labor Strikes

Role-Play 2

Homework

Task: Included are four sources about Germany during the Weimar Republic from 1919 to 1929. Imagine that they are actually about Nergmay. For a higher output grade, add details from these sources into your diary entry. And imagine that what is in these documents are things that you (your character) have actually seen.

The Basic Assignment: Write 1–2 paragraphs as a diary entry from your character's perspective about today's role-play.

- What did you (as the character) experience today? What were your reactions to the experience and your feelings about it?

- To what extent do the conditions in Nergmay help you achieve your hopes and dreams?

- Are you pleased or unpleased with the current conditions?

- How do you feel about the government's ability to create the type of society you want to live in?

Compelling Question: Is the government leading Nergmay in the right direction?

Output Grade	Amount of Output
1.	Do the basic assignment above.
2.	Close-Read sources A and B and make references to them in your diary entry.
3.	Close-read sources A, B, C, and D and incorporate details from them into your entry. Show how your character responds to the sources.

Output Grade	Amount of Output
4.	Close-read sources A, B, C, and D and incorporate details into your entry. Explain fully how your character views the role-play and reacts to the sources including thoughts and emotions, agreements and disagreements.

Source	Title or Author
A.	Mass Demonstration in Berlin's Lustgarten against the Treaty of Versailles (1919)[1]
B.	The Destruction of Heavy Weaponry after the Signing of the Treaty of Versailles (1919)[2]
C.	Butchering a Horse in the Streets of Berlin (1920)[3]
D.	Family Members Share a Single Sausage for Dinner (c.1920)[4]
Extension	Goldhagen, pp. 82–85.

Weimar and Nazi Germany 1: History of Anti-Semitism

The Gist: This initial role-play takes students back hundreds of years before the main role-play into the medieval manifestations of European anti-Semitism. The students, later, will ask why people hated the Jews. This single role-play cannot answer such a complex question, but it is a starting point for framing how hatred toward the other can evolve over time. We do this role-play before choosing characters so as not to confuse students about the time periods and the fact that this takes place centuries before the birth of their characters.

Homework #1: Anti-Semitism

Compelling Question: It is the year 1348. Thousands of people in your town have fallen sick to a plague. What should be your town's solution?

Source	Title or Author
A.	Black Death and the Burning of the Jews (image)[5]
B.	Top Ten Anti-Semitic Legends: Blood Libel (image)[6]
C.	Black Death and the Jews: The Cremation of Strasbourg Jewry, St. Valentine's Day[7]
D.	Expulsion of the Jews from France, 1182 CE[8]

Warm-up
What can make one group of people hate another group? List at least three possible reasons.

Scenery
Arrange a few desks in the back corner to make a well, leaving a space in the middle. I actually get a human anatomy model from a science class and I leave it on the ground, in that space.

Roles
At least seven Nergman townspeople: Henry, a Nergman townsperson (scene 1); Martin, a Wej (scene 1); Gregory, a Nergman miller and husband of Marta

(scene 2); Marta, Gregory's wife (scene 2); David, a Wejish tailor (scene 3); 2 Wej townspeople.

Suggested format
A fishbowl role-play with the above characters in the middle and the other students as observers, filling out a scaffolding worksheet. After each scene, I switch the role-players and the observers, making sure there are always far more Nergmans role-playing than Wejs.

Teacher Tip ✔

I like to start out the first role-play by giving observers the "artist" or "therapist" observation sheet. Periodically throughout we pause to see artist images or to hear what the therapists think the characters are thinking (and suggestions from them for how the character should think or act). I also put the following on the board:

Our imaginary world:

Nergmay	=	our country
Lerbin	=	our town/city
Nergmans	=	The majority of the people in Nergmay (99 percent) who follow the Tiashcrin religion
Wejs	=	A religious minority (1 percent)
Tiashcrin	=	the religion of most Nergmans

Background

It is the year 1300 in a small town that one day will become Lerbin. It is a world like that of the Middle Ages and you are all peasants. You work the land. You toil long days tilling the fields, planting, harvesting. You gather wood to cook.

It is the holiest day of the year. Most people in the town are native Nergmans who follow the religion of Tiashcrin. You go to your house of worship, drink wine, pray, and celebrate holidays with family. You do not like the Wejs. You have heard that years ago, in the beginning, corrupt Wejish leaders murdered your prince. You know that you have the "right" religion but the Wejs refuse to join you. They are different. They stick to their ways, to their own people. You still blame them for what their ancestors did to your prince. When things go wrong, you blame them. When sickness plagues the town, you are told it is their fault.

Scene 1: The Well

Teacher Reads

It is cold on this holy day. A Nergman townsperson, Henry, goes to the well to draw water. He uses the rope to lower the bucket. It seems to stick on something. He pulls harder and lifts the bucket. It is heavier than normal. It rises and he gasps. The bucket is holding a dead five-year-old boy.

Teacher Tip

If you have that anatomy model, put it in the well and then tell the students to "pull it out."

Choice Moment 1 (Henry)

You have found the body of a dead five-year-old boy in the well. What do you do?

Card 1A (Nergman Townsperson)

Oh no, it is little Thomas. He has been killed. It must have been a Wej. They are in alliance with the devil.

Choice Moment 2 (Henry)

Your fellow townsperson thinks it was a Wej who killed the boy. What do you do? (Have them discuss in small group, quietly)

Teacher Tip

Pause the action and ask therapists to describe the feelings and mindset of Henry and then of the Wejs who are observing this.

Card 1B (Nergman Townsperson)

I bet it was that Wej "Martin" Let's go get him!

Choice Moment 3 (all the Nergmans)

You've found the body and someone insists it was the Wej named Martin. What do you do?

Teacher Tip

I allow them to act out their choices as long as they are accurate in terms of weapons and technology. I stop them at certain points to hear from the artist and therapist observers.

Scene 2: The Mill

Teacher Reads

The year is 1350. It is a new generation of Nergmans but they have been taught the same things. The Nergmans like the Wejs no more than their grandparents did. They are still told that the Wejs were responsible for the prince's death and that they reject the true path.

It is the same holy day. A small Nergman miller, Gregory, and his wife, Marta, return from his house of worship and find their grain mill burned to the ground.

Choice Moment 4 (Gregory and Marta)

You have found your grain mill burned to the ground. What do you do?

Teacher Reads

They look closer, they run in to find the remains. They find bones. Somehow they know, they are the bones of their five sons.

Choice Moment 5 (Gregory and Marta)

You have found the bones of your five children in the ruins. What do you do?

Card 1C (Nergman Townsperson)

"Oh no, it is little Steven. It must have been a Wej. They are in alliance with the devil. I have heard that they use Tiashcrin blood for their rituals. They drink our children's blood!"

Choice Moment 6 (Gregory and Marta)

What do you do?

Scene 3: The Plague (Optional)

Teacher Reads

The year is 1400. It is a new generation of Nergmans but they have been taught the same things. The Nergmans like the Wejs no more than their grandparents did. They are still told that the Wejs were responsible for the prince's death and that they reject the true path.

People are not happy at this time. They are at the house of worship praying for themselves, for their loved ones. It is their only chance. People are dying and they don't know why. It is a plague. It is death. It is unstoppable. In the town hundreds die. Across the region, thousands. Across the land, millions. Pustules, gangrene, fever, pain and then, almost always, death.

After the service they walk to a well. They see a Wejish tailor, David, near the well, but he does not get water. He sees the group coming and walks away.

Choice Moment 7 (Nergman Townspeople)

What do you do?

Card 1D (Nergman Townsperson)

"I know why we are getting sick. That man poisoned the wells. The Wejs are poisoning our wells!"

Choice Moment 8 (David)

You see the Nergman townspeople, angry about the plague, talking about blaming Wejs. What do you do?

Weimar and Nazi Germany 2: Choosing a Character

The Gist: We choose characters on the second day because we will now be moving into the Weimar and Nazi eras. Students choose a role, they read the short paragraph about the character, and they use the character development sheet to add in possessions and skills.

Homework Debrief

It is the year 1348. Thousands of people in your town have fallen sick to a plague. What should be your town's solution?

Teacher Tip

Using their characters from yesterday, their experience in the role-play, and imagining that they've seen the images and scenarios from the homework sources, they make arguments to the council about what the town should do. I set up four or five chairs for townspeople making proposals and three chairs for town council members. I also jump in as a townsperson.

Character Choices

See tables on the next two pages.

1. Choose your character.

2. Choose three skills that would be helpful to you based on your character's job.

3. Choose two possessions that your character might need.

Role-Play Character Options

1. Dirk, a Nergman soldier.

2. Erhard, a Nergman policeman.

3. Dolf, a Nergman grocery store owner (dating Marisa).

4. Arnold, a Nergman police officer (married to Wilma).

5. Kurt, a Nergman baker (married to Marina).

6. Ulf, a Nergman clothing factory owner.

7. Rupert, a Nergman doctor.

8. Werner, a Nergman train conductor.

9. Thomas, Nergman priest.

10. Julius, a Nergman journalist.

11. Manfred, a Nergman factory worker.

12. Katharina, a Nergman teacher.

13. Hannah, Nergman works in clothing factory.

14. Therese, a Nergman teacher.

15. Wilma, a Nergman nurse (married to Arnold).

16. Marina, a Nergman illustrator (married to Kurt).

17. Sandra, a Nergman secretary (married to Leopold).

18. Simon, a Wejish history professor (married to Sophia).

19. Rachel, a Wejish teacher.

20. Gabriella, a Wejish homemaker (married to Joshua).

21. Sophia, a Wejish government official (married to Simon).

22. Joshua, a Wejish religious leader (married to Gabriella).

23. Michael, a Wejish grocery-store owner.

24. Stephen, a Wejish doctor and chairman of Wejish community.

25. Marisa, a Wejish nurse (dating Dolf).

26. Robert, a Wejish butcher.

27. Leopold, a Wejish metalworker (married to Sandra).

My character is: _____

Skills		
Carpentry	First aid	Skiing
Composing	Knowledge of science and	Stealth
Pottery/sculpture	history	Sewing
Woodcarving	Theater	Public speaking
Forgery	Picking a lock	Drawing
Climbing	Cooking	Math
Repairing broken items	Card tricks	Memory
Writing	Swimming	Gymnastics
Boxing	Running	Handling animals
Bargaining	Hiking	Nature survival
	Musical instruments	
	Singing	

My three skills are:

1. _____ 2. _____ 3. _____

Equipment		
Book of prayers	Saw	A diamond ring and
Camouflage clothes	Hammer and nails	necklace
Climbing boots	Winter boots	A typewriter
Compass, magnetic	Kayak	A sewing machine
Drill	Book of matches	Saddle
Rope	Magnets	Skis
Violin	Calligraphy set	Snowshoes
Fur clothing	Paints	Cooking knives
Suitcase with false bottom	Paper and pens	Ice skates
Ladder	Pistol (police officers)	Suit
Cards		Backpack
First-aid kit		Large suitcase
		Two water bottles

My two possessions are:

1. _____ 2. _____

Character Sheet

Character Name _____	Character Job _____
Skills: Copy from previous page 1. _____ 2. _____ 3. _____	**Equipment**: Copy from previous page 1. _____ 2. _____

Race/nationality: _____

Gender: _____

Languages: _____

Religion: _____

Attributes

Assign the following numbers to the six attributes below: 13, 11, 7, 12, 8, 4 points.

Force   ___   Dexterity   ___   Perception   ___

Health   ___   Intelligence   ___   Interpersonal   ___

Force	=	Brute physical strength.
Health	=	Physical health and ability to withstand and recover from injury.
Dexterity	=	Quickness, skill with hands, agility.
Intelligence	=	Smartness.
Perception	=	Ability to make good decisions.
Interpersonal	=	Strong charisma, ability to convince others to take your point of view.

At this point make a name-tag for your character, which should include all the key information that is above.

The Characters

Note: Full character descriptions are available online at:
http://davidsherrin.wix.com/davidsherrin

Dirk, a Nergman soldier: You are a 22-year-old former soldier who fought bravely in the Grand War. You believed in defending your country's interests and reputation and you saw many of your friends die in battle. The loss of the war hurt you deeply. You gained pride in what it meant to be Nergman during the war and to lose meant to take something away from your soul. You wish you knew whom to blame for Nergmay's loss. You aren't totally sure what you will do after the war. Sometimes you have memories of it. You remember the fear and the excitement. Coming back to a city where no one seems to care what you went through is disappointing. You're actually not sure what success means to you as a person but you think it begins with finding a job. Your ultimate success mission is to rebuild your country's pride and make Nergmay what it once was: a superpower.

Erhard, a Nergman policeman: You are a 24-year-old former soldier. You fought in the Grand War because that it what you were supposed to do. When Nergmay goes to war, your family does its part. Your grandfather fought in some of the great wars of old. You didn't particularly think the war made sense or was worth it. There were too many deaths and injuries. For what? But you did your duty and that is what counts. Once you returned to your hometown you did what made sense: you got a job as a policeman to use what you learned from the war. You care about doing everything well, including your job. If you are a policeman now, you want to be the best one you can be. You believe in the Social Democratic Party that runs the country. It is moderate and cautious. Some people have even suggested you should use your war record to run for local or national office. Your success mission is to advance in your career, to find a wife, to have a family, and to feel like you've done your part for your city.

Dolf, a Nergman grocery-store owner (dating Marisa)
Arnold, a Nergman police officer (married to Wilma)
Kurt, a Nergman baker (married to Marina)
Ulf, a Nergman clothing factory owner
Rupert, a Nergman doctor
Julius, a Nergman journalist
Werner, a Nergman train conductor
Thomas, Nergman priest
Manfred, a Nergman factory worker

Katharina, a Nergman teacher
Hannah, Nergman works in clothing factory
Therese, a Nergman teacher
Wilma, a Nergman nurse (married to Arnold)
Marina, a Nergman illustrator (married to Kurt)
Sandra, a Nergman secretary (married to Leopold)

Simon, a Wejish history professor (married to Sophia): At the beginning of this role-play, you are a 33-year-old history professor at the leading university of the city. Being a Wej is a significant part of your life. You study about Wejish history and you write (and teach) about the history of the Wej people in Nergmay. You grew up in a religious family and still attend the house of worship where Barib Joshua is the leader. However, you consider yourself between two worlds: the religious and the academic. Living the life of a Wej, to some degree, is important to you as is the community. However, you also care deeply about the intellectual world, about new ideas, modernity, and the opinion of your fellow Nergman professors. You are up for tenure to achieve lifetime security as a professor at the university. Your success mission is to continue to participate in the Wej community, to publish books, to gain a higher position in the university, and to have children.

Rachel, a Wejish teacher: You are a 31-year-old elementary school teacher. You are a secular (non-religious) Wej who has a passion for the Wejish people and their history, but not for the religion. You belong to the Wejish people, but you consider many of the ancient religious traditions and prayers to be outdated. Recently you have become part of a secret group of Wejs who dream of re-establishing a Wejish homeland in Wejistan, the ancient faraway land of your people. There, you could govern yourselves and be free of any possible persecution. Family life means little to you right now. Your success mission is to to help get Wejs out of Nergmay and to the land of Wejistan, where you could fight for its independence from foreign control.

Gabriella, a Wejish homemaker
Sophia, a Wejish government official (married to Simon)
Barib Joshua, a Wejish religious leader
Michael, a Wejish grocery-store owner
Dr. Stephen, a Wejish doctor and chairman of Wejish community
Marisa, a Wejish nurse (dating Dolf)
Robert, a Wejish butcher
Leopold, a Wejish metalworker (married to Sandra)

Weimar and Nazi Germany 3: Unemployment and Labor Strikes

The Gist: Today, the students become their characters and we begin to explain why Germany became a country ripe for fascism and a place where a weak democracy would vote the Nazi Party into power.

Homework #2: Unemployment

Compelling Question: Is the government leading Nergmay in the right direction?

Source	Title or Author
A.	Mass Demonstration in Berlin's Lustgarten against the Treaty of Versailles (1919)[9]
B.	The Destruction of Heavy Weaponry after the Signing of the Treaty of Versailles (1919)[10]
C.	Butchering a Horse in the Streets of Berlin (1920)[11]
D.	Family Members Share a Single Sausage for Dinner (c. 1920)[12]
Extension	Goldhagen, pp. 82–85.

Warm-up

Option 1: What do you remember about life in Nergmay from our first role-play?

Option 2: What was the relationship like between Nergmans and Wejs in our first role-play? What seemed to cause those feelings and what were two consequences of those feelings?

Background

About seven hundred years have passed since the first role-play. Nergmay is a modern country now with scientists, libraries, electricity, and public schools. We are in the twentieth century. Life has changed a great deal for the Wejs, who make up about 1 percent of the population. They are a welcome part of the society and four out of five Wejs are Nergman citizens. They have freedom of religion and they hold government jobs; they are doctors and lawyers, teachers and scientists. Many have lost touch with the traditional Wejish religion. Many consider themselves more Nergman than Wejish. Some, like Barib Joshua hold on to tradition. Many Wejs, however, barely even recognize that part of who they are.

Nergmay has just been through a brutal war with neighboring countries. The Grand War is over and the soldiers are coming home to your city of Lerbin. Nergmay was defeated. Soldiers like Dirk, Arnold, and Erhard thought the Grand War would be an adventure. But it was hell. Brothers died, friends died. Soldiers lost legs. Eyes stopped working. Arnold was a war hero but now he has headaches. Erhard can't sleep. And Dirk, it is so painful for him to walk. For what? The treaty that ended the war was the ultimate humiliation. Nergmans were told that they were wrong, to blame, guilty. The Nergmans are responsible, the treaty says. Nergmans must pay.

During the war, there was sacrifice at home, too. Women took the place of men at factories, working long hours. There were shortages of bread and milk. Children went hungry. War-wounded are all over: men without limbs, without sight, begging. Many are homeless. And many whisper that the problem was the treaty. Why should we pay the countries we lost to? You know whose fault it really is, they say. The Wejs. Those dirty Wejs, they start to whisper. They're responsible for the lost war. The Wejs stabbed us in the back.

The soldiers coming home see a different city than what they had left. The city feels free, alive, vibrant. There is a zoo, the lakes are sparkling, and streetcars and double-decker buses rush through the avenues. The culture is intense, dynamic. Women seem to have more freedom and elegance, a new style, and new hopes for the future.

But times are tough. Munitions factories have closed since there is no need for guns or ammunition. Thousands of workers lost their jobs. Women were told to leave jobs for returning soldiers. With the economy so bad, Dirk, Leopold and Werner cannot find jobs. After men returned from the front, Marisa, Sandra and Therese lost theirs.

All over the city people are angry. There are strikes—of miners and factory workers. They say they are getting paid too little. They stand outside and demand more.

Scene 1: The Café

Scenery
Try to have a few signs that say "we want more pay" or "value your workers" or some other slogan a picketing worker might use. Arrange a few desks in the back of the room that will be the factory.

Role-Players

Dirk, Leopold, Werner, Marisa, Sandra, Therese.

Teacher Reads

Dirk, Leopold, Werner, Marisa, Sandra, and Therese are at a café. You all know each other from your neighborhood. It is a nice summer, the breeze has cooled things down, and you need to decide where to go. There is so much to do in Lerbin but you have no money to do it.

A man in his early thirties, with wavy brown hair, and intense brown eyes walks up to you. He knows Dirk from the war. They were in the same regiment. He sits next to you.

Teacher Tip

You can choose one student to play this temporary NPC (non-player character) role or you can play it.

Card 3A (Man)

Where do you work?

Card 3B (Man)

The people who have jobs don't appreciate what they have. I've heard there are people right now, who work at a clothes factory, who are on strike. They want more money. They stand around outside the shoe factory, just holding signs. Imagine if you could get by and speak to the owner, Ulf. You could offer to work for what the owner pays them or even a little less. Get a job, you know. These other people don't deserve what they have.

Choice Moment 1
(Dirk, Leopold, Werner, Marisa, Sandra, Therese)

The man is suggesting you try to break the picket line to get a job at the clothes factory. What do you do? Why?

Teacher Tip

If students decide to try to get past the picketers, give them a few moments (or minutes) to come up with a plan. How will they get by? I either ask them to step to the corner to come up with a plan or to step outside the room for 3–4 minutes.

Scene 2: Outside the Factory

Role-Players

- Strike-breakers: Dirk, Leopold, Werner, Marisa, Sandra, Therese.
- Picketers: Manfred and Hannah plus 1–4 other students who can take NPC roles.
- The police officers (Erhard, Arnold) are stationed outside.
- Choose 1–3 other characters (like a doctor or nurse) to be bystanders who can get involved depending on what happens.
- You may want Julius (journalist) and Marina (illustrator) to be recording the scene.

Teacher Reads
They arrive at the factory and find a picket line with about 30 people there, holding signs. Manfred and Hannah are there picketing due to unfair working conditions. Dirk, Leopold, Werner, Marisa, Sandra, and Therese walk up toward them.

Card 3C (Manfred and Hannah)

"We want our just pay; we are workers not slaves!"

Choice Moment 2
(Dirk, Leopold, Werner, Marisa, Sandra, Therese)

You are outside the factory and you see people picketing. What do you do?

Teacher Tip

Here students need to decide whether to fight, to sneak by, or to negotiate to get inside the factory. This year, my students pretended to join the strike in solidarity and then succeeded in sneaking by unnoticed. You need to ask those on strike (Manfred and Hannah) to pretend that they did not witness the previous discussion in the club.

Depending on the response, see how other bystanders nearby respond. The police? A doctor? How do the picketers respond? There might be violence, which should be allowed to take place. There could be negotiations or trickery. At times, I've had students get by them; other times they fail to do so. Remember, there is always the 20-sided die to resolve any conflicts.

Scene 3

(Optional—If They Make it Inside the Factory)

Role-Players
Whoever makes it inside the factory, plus Ulf, the factory owner.

Teacher Reads
There are only a few lights on. It is dark, with a musty smell of human sweat. You see the machines, big machines, and all the cotton fabric. You can see this place makes money. The officer door is closed. You knock.

Card 3D (Ulf)

"Come in."
(Look angry and annoyed at them; you're not happy to be bothered.)

Card 3E (Ulf)

What do you want? Can't you see I'm busy? Does it look like I'm on vacation?

Choice Moment 3 (Dirk, Werner, Therese, and Marisa)

What do you say to the factory owner? What do you propose to him?

Teacher Tip

In order to create conflict, you might want to tell Ulf he can only hire a couple of the potential workers and he can only pay them 50–75 percent of what the normal workers make. It is nice to give him freedom to negotiate, but if you want, you can also just give him card 3F.

Card 3F (Ulf)

I can only hire two of you. Who here needs a job more? But I'll only pay you 80 percent of the normal wages.

Choice Moment 4 (Dirk, Werner, Therese, and Marisa)

What do you do? Who will take the job? Will you take the job for less money?

Weimar and Nazi Germany 4: Weimar Inflation

The Gist: Through a look at hyperinflation, this session cements the notion that there were serious economic and social problems in Weimar Germany that led to considerable discontent and unrest.

Homework #3: Inflation

Compelling Question: Is the government leading Nergmay in the right direction?

Source	Title or Author
A.	Line Outside of a Berlin Grocer (1923)[13]
B.	Wallpapering with Worthless Banknotes (1923)[14]
C.	Friedrich Kroner, "Overwrought Nerves" (1923)[15]
D.	Striped Bathing Suit (1925)[16] and In the "Eldorado" Transvestite Bar on Motzstrasse, Berlin (1926)[17]

Warm-up

Option 1: Look carefully at the image from Source B from your homework for tonight. Describe three specific things you see in the image.

Option 2: What are two problems in Nergmay right now?

Teacher Tip

This role-play requires a good amount of set-up. Ahead of time, I print out pictures of Weimar currency as well as three photographs of milk, 2 of cereal, 2 of bread, 1 of steak, and 1 of a toy car. I hand those images to the store owners as they are making their store signs. I also print copies of the buying chart to give to each of the purchasers (along with the right amount of cash) and a selling chart to each of the store owners.

Set up Dolf, Kurt/Marina, Michael, and Robert at the stores. Dolf owns a grocery store; Kurt and Marina own a bakery; Michael owns a grocery store; Robert owns a butcher shop.

Give them printed out pictures of milk, steak, cereal, bread, and a toy car according to the amount they have in the "store chart." Make sure they each have a few billion karms to use as change. Explain to them (in secret) that prices are going up and they want to sell at the price indicated on the chart.

Hand all the buyers the Buying Chart. Explain that they should look at what they need to buy, the price of that item yesterday, and the amount of money that they have.

Ask Stephen, Simon, Ulf, Sandra, and Marisa to go first and then the other buyers to line up behind them.

Background

It has been one year since the strike at Ulf's clothing factory. Life since the war has not been easy. The treaty hit Nergmay hard. You were blamed for the war and forced to pay. The winners had no mercy. Your country has had to pay more than a billion karms to the winner. But there just aren't jobs to create that money and the people refuse to increase taxes. They don't have the money. Poverty seems to wear the people down as they wander through empty days. They walk slower, their backs start to stoop. Some just seem to stare into the distance.

The government, called the Reimaw Government, is a democracy with a constitution, free and equal suffrage, proportional voting, and basic political liberties. Led by the Social Democratic Party, there is health insurance, pensions, and an eight-hour work day. Women can vote. Some people consider the government to be too weak. It can't protect the borders. Neighboring countries have moved troops into Nergmay, seizing industrial cities and coal mines.

The leaders keep coming and going. No one can stay in power. In order to pay off the foreign countries, the government has just printed more money. And more money. And more money. But now it is worth less on the street. It is like water . . . if you keep pouring it out, no one needs it anymore. It is just paper. Communists stage an armed uprising—often labor unrest and strikes happen on the streets.

Too much money has led to hyperinflation. It is worth nothing. A year ago a carton of milk cost 10 karms. Two months ago it cost 100 karms. A month ago it cost 2,000 karms. A week ago it cost 6 million karms. Yesterday a carton of milk cost 2 billion karms.[18]

People are not happy. You hear them talking openly on the street. This is the fault of the peace treaty, they declare. And you know who was behind that . . . the Wejs, they say. They talked about breaking "the Wejish domination of the state."

In the past year, some of you have significant changes to your life. Manfred returned to work in the factory but Hannah lost her job in the strike. Ulf has also hired Leopold to maintain his machines. Dirk has found a job as a police officer and the government hired Werner to run a train line. Therese still does not have a job and has moved home with her parents. Sandra and Leopold have just had a baby boy.

For strong performance in the previous role-play in taking on their persona and/or achieving success, the following characters may choose one new skill: _____.

For completing the homework and/or debriefing it, the following characters earn +1 point for interpersonal: _____.

Scene 1: At the Stores

Scenery and Set-up
Set up a row of three desks to the side of the room to make it seem to be a row of stores. Ask the store owners to make a sign for their store that says "Butcher Shop," "Grocery Store," and "Bakery." Tape the signs to the front of the table.

Suggested Role-Players

- Store owners: Dolf, Kurt/Marina, Michael, and Robert.
- Shoppers: Ulf, Rupert, Thomas, Katharina, Manfred, Therese, Werner, Marisa, Wilma, Sandra, Simon, Gabriella, Sophia, Stephen, Leopold.
- Police officers: Erhard, Arnold.

Teacher Does
This role-play should be fluid; allow students to buy and sell their items. Based on the suggested buying and selling prices, there will be conflict either because the price is too high or there is not enough stock. Ask the characters to consider their options when the exchanges become difficult. They might decide to leave in frustration, to attempt to steal, to trade something they have (barter), to join their funds together to buy something, to beat up the store owner, to riot, or to sneak in the back.

Teacher Tip

Depending on a student's action, consider asking them their role. This year a student decided to stab someone on the street for bread. When I stopped her, I found out she was Dr. Stephen. We read the role-card for Dr. Stephen out loud and then I asked for a vote on whether the action was plausible given Dr. Stephen's biography. They voted no and the student had to revise her action.

Table 5.2 Inflation Buying Chart

Character	What wants to buy	Price 1 month ago	Price yesterday	How much money has to spend
Ulf	Milk	1,000 karms	2 billion karms	3 billion karms
Rupert	Cereal	1,000 karms	2 billion karms	1 billion karms
Werner	Bread	500 karms	1 billion karms	1/2 billion karms
Thomas	Bread	500 karms	1 billion karms	1/2 billion karms
Manfred	Milk	1,000 karms	2 billion karms	1 billion karms
Katharina	Steak	2,000 karms	4 billion karms	4 billion karms
Wilma	Cereal	1,000 karms	2 billion karms	2 billion karms
Therese	Milk for child Bread for child	1,000 karms 500 karms	2 billion karms 1 billion karms	4 billion karms
Simon	Toy car for child for holiday	1,000 karms	3 billion karms	5 billion karms
Sandra	Milk for child	1,000 karms	2 billion karms	1 billion karms
Gabriella	Bread	500 karms	1 billion karms	1 billion karms
Sophia	Steak	2,000 karms	4 billion karms	2 billion karms
Leopold	Steak	2,000 karms	4 billion karms	3 billion karms
Stephen	Cereal	1,000 karms	2 billion karms	3 billion karms
Marisa	Toy car for child for holiday	1,000 karms	3 billion karms	4 billion karms

Table 5.3 Inflation Selling Chart

What to Sell	Quantity in Stock	Price to Sell
Milk (grocery)	Dolf: 2 Michael: 1	3 billion karms
Cereal (grocery)	Dolf: 0 Michael: 2	3 billion karms
Bread (bakery)	Kurt: 2	2 billion karms
Steak (butcher)	Robert: 1	6 billion karms
Toy car for child (grocery)	Dolf: 1	5 billion karms

All these are legitimate choices that may be role-played. At that point, you might consider bringing in one or two police officers. How do they respond? Are they honest? Do they ask for bribes to help the store owners? What do the characters do when the store runs out of inventory of a particular item?

After role-playing these interactions for a while, I often have a student who has left the store unable to purchase groceries run into an older man on the street carrying a bag of groceries. This becomes a choice moment for that character: does he or she help the man or steal the groceries?

There are many scenarios you can throw in depending on time. What if they see a beggar on the street? What do the police officers do if there is violence? What if the owner gives food to a friend for a lower price? What do the people on line do?

Weimar and Nazi Germany 5: Weimar Great Depression

The Gist: This is the third pre-election role-play meant to solidify an understanding of the major economic problems in Weimar Germany and the desperation prevalent in much of Weimar society. This is crucial for students to understand why the Nazi Party won a plurality in the national election.

Homework #4: The Great Depression

Compelling Question: What are Nergmay's problems? Who can provide a better solution: The Social Democratic Party or the Sizan Party?

A Special Assignment: Tomorrow we will have an election between Ulf or Rupert (running for the Sizan Party) and Erhard or Dolf (for the Social Democratic Party). Write one or two paragraphs as a **diary entry or speech** from your character's perspective.

- Ulf or Rupert: Write a one-page speech about why you and the Sizan Party offer a better solution.
- Erhard or Dolf: Write a one-page speech about why you and the Social Democratic Party offer a better solution.
- Julius: Write a one-page newspaper editorial supporting one of the parties and candidates and explaining why this election is important.
- Marina: You have been hired by the Sizan Party to make two propaganda illustrations supporting the Sizan Party. Make those illustrations.
- Everyone else: Write your diary entry about the compelling question and your thoughts on the upcoming election. Consider questions you might ask the candidates.

Source	Title or Author
A.	Unemployed Stenotypist Seeks Work (December 1931);[19] Homeless Men's Shelter (date unknown) (Economics—1929–1933: Depression)[20]
B.	Sizan (Nazi) Party Platform[21]
C.	Social Democratic Party Platform[22]
D.	Betty Scholem on the Depression (August 1931)[23]

Oliver
David and Miles
Genocide and Justice
2/27/15

Sizan Party Speech

Hello citizens of Nergmay.

I stand here today to bringing you a union, to forms a single great country of Nergmay. The first thing we will do, is abolish the war treaty. We will not, and cannot continue to pay the debt which is ruining our country. We stand for a sound, and prosperous middle-class. The Sizan Party believes that the state has a duty to help raise the standard of national health by providing maternity welfare centers and increasing the physical fitness of the population.

We need a complete reconstruction of our national system of education. We will have programs to help specially talented children with poor parents what ever their station or occupation to be educated at the expense of the state so that Nergmay's most talented and brilliant future engineers, scientists, mathematicians, athletes, teachers, politicians, and artists are not left to die never knowing their greatness and sharing it with the rest of the world.

Good citizenship shall be taught from the beginning. Nergman blood is a requirement for Nergman citizenship. We demand freedom for all religious faiths in the state as long as they do not endanger its existence or offend the moral and ethical sense of the Nergmanic race. No foreigners or Wejs can be a member of the nation. The wealth of Nergmay may should go to Nergmans.

No further immigration of non-Nergman's. Any non-Nergman who entered Nergmay after August 2, 1914, shall leave. Foreigners living in Nergmay only as noncitizens, are subject to the law of aliens. The state shouldn't share every citizen lives decently and earns his livelihood. If it is impossible to provide food for the whole population, then noncitizens must be expelled to take care of Nergmans. All newspapers in Nergmay, must be published by Nergman citizens and owners. We need more land and territory for our surplus population. We need to show how great we are and not cower under lesser nations. We will make a greater Nergmay. Long live Nergmay!

Figure 5.1 Oliver's Homework

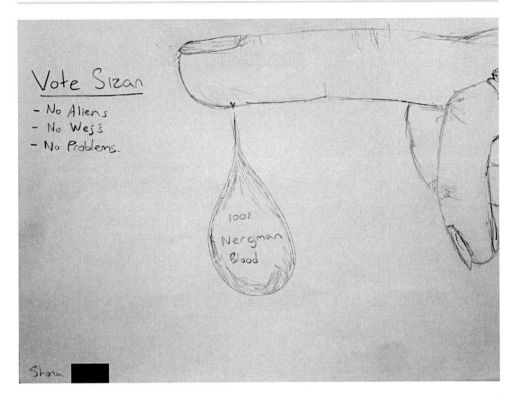

Figure 5.2 Shona's PDD Homework Preparation

Warm-up

Option 1: Look at the images for Source A in your homework for tonight. Describe three specific things that you see in the image.

Option 2: Vocabulary matching review.

Table 5.4 Example of a Vocabulary Matching Review

A. Inflation	1. The deliberate killing of a large group of people, especially those of a particular ethnic group or nation.
B. Anti-Semitism	2. When a person who is actively searching for employment is unable to find work.
C. Unemployment	3. Hostility to or prejudice against Jews.
D. Genocide	4. A general increase in prices and fall in the purchasing value of money.
E. Weimar Republic	5. The democratic government founded in Germany after the end of World War I.

Background

Seven years have passed since the terrible inflation. The Reimaw government continues to be stuck in a spiral of instability. There has been unemployment, inflation and constant changes of government. No one trusts the government any more. They can't fix your problems. After a stock market crash across the ocean, a terrible depression has struck Nergmay. Economic and social conditions are even worse.

Banks have failed and people have lost their entire life savings.

Unemployment is rampant. People are on the streets begging, people who once lived a typical middle-class lifestyle. The government has cut down on its workforce and businesses like banks and stores have eliminated jobs.

This depression has hit you. Sandra, Werner, Rachel, Leopold, Arnold, Manfred, Katharina, and Hannah have all lost their jobs. Arnold and Wilma had their first child two years ago, a baby boy. They are living with Wilma's parents. Both unemployed, Sandra and Leopold have to share a rented apartment with another couple in a dirty, somewhat dangerous building. Marina and Kurt had a baby boy. His bakery is doing well and they moved into a lovely two-bedroom apartment. Marisa stopped dating Dolf and is now together with Manfred and they have gotten pretty serious.

For strong performance in the previous role-play in taking on their persona and/or achieving success, the following characters may choose one new possession (unless they are unemployed): _____.

For completing the homework and/or debriefing it, the following characters earn +1 point for dexterity: _____.

Scene 1: The Breakfast

Role-players
Arnold, Wilma, son (NPC).

Set-up and Scenery
I arrange three chairs in the middle for Arnold, Wilma, and their son to sit around an imaginary table.

Teacher Reads
It is morning in the home of Arnold and Wilma. Arnold has nowhere to go that day. He has no job. Wilma's pay has been reduced. She looks at her husband at the breakfast table. She looks at her two-year-old son. "Hungry"

their son says. He starts to cry. She looks at the food at the table. There is one sausage on the plate—for all three of them to share.

Choice Moment 1 (Wilma)

What do you say to Arnold?

Choice Moment 2 (Arnold)

How do you respond to Wilma?

Teacher Tip

If they are having trouble jump-starting the conversation, just remind them of the difficulties they are facing and ask them to have a discussion about their options. This year, they discussed their difficulties and Wilma said how Arnold needed to get a job. He looked devastated. When the conversation stalled, it became a great moment to pause and go to suggestions and insights from the observers.

Scene 2: Michael's Store (Optional)

Role-Players
Michael, Arnold, Stephen, Leopold.

Teacher Reads
After his conversation with Wilma, Arnold decides to go to Michael's store to ask him for a job. He is desperate. He thinks carefully about the argument he can use to persuade the grocery-store owner. What can he offer? When he arrives, he sees he is not alone. Leopold, a young man who had previously been a metalworker, is also there searching for a job. He also notices Dr. Stephen, the well-known head of the Wejish Community Board, shopping in the store.

Choice Moment 3 (Arnold)

What do you say to Michael?

Choice Moment 4 (Leopold)

What do you say to Michael?

Choice Moment 5 (Dr. Stephen)

You overhear the conversation and walk over. What do you do or say?

Choice Moment 6 (Michael)

You have heard the requests. You can only offer one job. Do you have other questions? Who do you offer the job to?

Scene 2: The Cabaret (Optional)

Role-Players

Sandra, Werner, Rachel, Leopold, Arnold, Manfred, Katharina, Hannah.

Teacher Reads

The strange thing about this city is that so many people are miserable but the city is still alive. It is one o'clock in the afternoon and those of you without jobs (Sandra, Werner, Rachel, Leopold, Arnold, Manfred, Katharina, and Hanna) have gone to a cabaret called Waterland. It is a place to forget your troubles. It is a five-story nightclub that fits 6,000 diners. There is a Wild West bar with waiters in cowboy hats and a wine terrace. It is a fun night-club with singing and dancing. You want to relax and have some fun and forget the difficulties.

Teacher Tip

At this point I pass out lyrics to the song "It's a Swindle" and I play a video of the song. Both are easily available on the Internet. We briefly step out of character to discuss what the song is saying about life in Reimaw.

Werner turns to the rest of you. You know each other from high school, from work, and from the cabaret.

Card 5A (Werner)

We need to do something. I can't go home without food again. I can't go home without money or a job. I have a wife now. What do we do? I'm going to change my life today. I can't keep going on like this.

Choice Moment 7 (Everyone)

What do you do? What are your options?

Teacher Tip

Have students consider their options. Perhaps they try to swindle, to steal, or to find a job. If they want to do that have them come up with a plan and try to act it out.

Weimar and Nazi Germany 6:
The Election PDD

The Gist: This lesson helps us grasp why the German people, in a state of crisis, voted the Nazi Party into power in a free and fair election. It is important to note that the Nazis did not win a majority of the vote, but in a multi-party system won the plurality. This is the first PDD of the unit and it asks students to advocate for a particular direction in Nergman politics.

Our Main Question: Who will fix the problems of Nergmay: Erhard or Dolf and the Social Democratic Party, or the Sizan Party's candidates, Ulf or Rupert?

Homework #5: The Election

Compelling Question: Has Nergmay moved in the right direction since the election?

Source	Title or Author
A.	SA Members Arrest Communists in Berlin on the Day after the Reichstag Elections[24]
B.	The Reichswehr Swears an Oath of Allegiance to Adolf Hitler on the Day of Hindenburg's Death[25]
C.	Decree of the Reich President for the Protection of the People and State[26]
D.	Law for the Restoration of the Professional Civil Service[27]

Warm-up
Option 1: Prepare for the Pivotal Decision Debate (see format below).

Option 2: List the three most difficult parts about life in Nergmay for your character.

Homework Debrief
This takes place through the election debate.

Teacher Tip

It is worth explaining the roles for today's PDD at the beginning of class and giving students 5–15 minutes to prepare for their parts. The debaters should write down their main points and review their speeches. The audience should think of comments and questions they would like to make during the debate. Julius and Marina ought to copy their article and propaganda images to disperse to the class.

Format of the Pivotal Decision Debate

1. Preparation: Everyone has 15 minutes to prepare.
2. Candidates for the same party should share their ideas, strategize, and help each other with the speeches. Candidates should make sure they are familiar with their party platform and ways to highlight weaknesses in the other party.
3. Citizens should read over the newspaper article, illustrations, and party platforms. Each citizen should prepare a one-sentence statement and one question for each of the candidates.
4. Debate speeches: 4 minutes each.
5. Statements and questions from the audience (answers from the candidates): 10–20 minutes.
6. The vote.

Background

About 30 percent of the population in Nergmay is unemployed. The disagreements in government mean that no solutions are being brought forward. Society is fragmented. Due to reparation payments it must make, Nergmay is hit particularly hard during a depression.

One new political party has emerged in the past decade, filled with young people. It is called the Sizan Party and there is a feeling of energy within it. They stand on the streets with pamphlets and propaganda posters, handing out their message. They exude a sense of strength.

The government, meanwhile, has fired civil servants and is cutting unemployment benefits. Over 5 million people are without work.

An election is about to be held. You have the sense that this election is crucial for Nergmay; it could change it forever. You need to decide who to vote for.

Each of you has before you a copy of the Party Platforms of the Sizan Party and the Social Democratic Party. The Social Democrats have ruled Nergmay democratically throughout this period since the Grand War. The Sizan Party is relatively new to Nergmay's political scene. The President of Nergmay recently appointed the Sizan's charismatic leader, Terhil, as Chancellor of the country, putting most of the power in his hands. There has been a recent increase in violence with police attacking the meetings of the Social Democratic Party.

Policemen loyal to Terhil march through the streets. Some of the Social Democrat's leading politicians have left the country. Six days before the election, a main government building burned down. After the fire, to ensure public safety, the government passed an emergency law taking away freedom of the press and assembly. Some people critical of Terhil have been imprisoned; some newspapers critical of the Sizan Party have been shut down.

You all arrive for a debate at the grand municipal hall. There are candidates running for national office as deputies of Nergmay's Congress. They are representing their political parties: the Sizan Party and the Social Democratic Party.

The Social Democratic Party has two candidates on the ballot: Erhard, a former soldier, and Dolf. For the Sizan Party are Rupert and Ulf. Each will have four minutes to give a speech outlining what they and their party will do to solve Nergmay's problems and bring the country to a better future. At that point, they will take questions from the audience for 10 minutes and audience members will have 10 minutes to make their own arguments about Nergmay's election. Then, we will vote in this critical Nergman election between the Social Democrats and the Sizan Party. You are voting for a political party, not a candidate.

For strong performance in the previous role-play in taking on their persona and/or achieving success, the following characters may choose to fulfill one of their personal goals (such as marriage): _____.

For completing the homework and/or debriefing it, the following characters earn +1 point for health: _____.

Scene 1: The Debate

Teacher Reads
Newspapers and pamphlets spread throughout the streets of Lerbin discussing the importance of the upcoming election for the future of the Nergman people. One newspaper with a growing influence is *The Thunderstorm*. You gather in the halls of the municipal building to hear the candidates debate and to share your views.

Teacher Tip

Follow the protocol of this PDD. At the end, students should fill out the ballots and you may tally. I have always found the Sizan (Nazi) Party to win but since they are voting for one particular deputy the Social Democratic candidate can win and we still have the Sizan Party win the larger national election. I give them a ballot that looks like this.

Note: Additional Nergman Election Ballots can be found online at: http://davidsherrin.wix.com/davidsherrin. Party platforms for the Social Democratic Party and the Sizan Party can be found online at: http://davidsherrin.wix.com/davidsherrin

Table 5.5 Nergmay Election Ballot for Congressional Deputy

Candidates	Political Party	Place check in this box to vote for the candidate
Erhard and Dolf	Social Democratic Party	
Ulf and Rupert	Sizan Party	

Weimar and Nazi Germany 7: Book Burning and Boycotts

The Gist: This role-play brings out the increased persecution (the tightening net) around the Jews after Hitler's accession to power in Nazi Germany. Students should begin to understand how state policy and civilian acquiescence can lead to systematic discrimination against a group.

Homework #6: Book Burnings and Boycotts

Compelling Question: How did Germany change after the election?

Source	Title or Author
A.	SA Members in Front of the Tietz Department Store in Berlin (April 1, 1933)[28]
B.	Against the Un-German Spirit: Book-Burning Ceremony in Berlin[29]
C.	SS Marriage Order (December 31, 1931)[30]
D.	Victor Klemperer's Diary Entry on the Impending Boycott of Jewish Businesses (March 31, 1933)[31]
Extension, Secondary Source	Zeller, pp. 23–37.

Warm-up

Option 1: Why do you think the Sizan Party won the election? What do you think the people who voted for them want the Sizan Party to do?

Option 2: Take six minutes and read Source D from your homework for tonight. What does it tell you about life in Nergmay since the election?

Background

The Sizan Party is in power. In the election, the Sizans won about 37 percent of the vote among many parties, so they won the most amount of seats.

Many Nergmans have earned jobs from the new government, especially the unemployed police officers who now work in security for the state.

After Terhil took over, the country experienced a wave of state-sponsored violence. Terhil's police officers arrested, beat, and killed people they considered enemies of the state, including communists and Wejs. They created prisons and torture stations in places like basements and garages.

The government placed the press under its control with near total censorship.

Sizan flags are everywhere. Sizan parades are everywhere. There is a sense that a new era has come.

At the urging of the Sizan office of propaganda, the Sizan Nergman Student Association has declared a nationwide "Action against the Un-Nergman Spirit" for May 10.

Many of your own lives have changed considerably. The police department hired Arnold while Dirk earned a promotion to sergeant. Erhard, however, has been demoted in rank. The economy has picked up. New factories have been built and Leopold earned a job at a metalworking plant and Hannah at a clothing factory. The government has increased hiring, and Werner and Sandra both gained government employment. Rachel and Katharina finally began teaching at a local school. Only Manfred continues to look desperately for a job. Simon and Sophia had a baby boy and Joshua and Gabriella had twin girls.

For strong performance in the previous role-play in taking on their persona and/or achieving success, the following characters may choose one new possession (unless they are unemployed): _____.

For completing the homework and/or debriefing it, the following characters earn +1 point for dexterity: _____.

All Wejs lose 1 interpersonal point.

Scene 1: Book Burnings

Role-play characters
Dirk, Erhard, Arnold, Ulf, Julius, Werner, Thomas, Katharina, Wilma, Marina, Simon, Rachel, Barib Joshua, Sophia, Dr. Stephen.

Setting
I clear a space in the middle of the room and I place a pile of books there, on the floor, without telling the students why.

Teacher Reads

It is a Saturday night in early fall. The wind is beginning to whip through the trees as the sun sets over the buildings to your left. You are walking down the street to go to a restaurant. You see a parade of college students carrying torches. You see a crowd gathering near some light that is flickering. The head of a local university and a leading Sizan official are speaking to the crowd. You realize the head of the national Sizan Party's propaganda office is there. He yells, "I consign to the flames these books" and throws two of them in. There must be about 40,000 people there. You notice police officers: Dirk, Erhard, and Arnold are standing at the edge. There is a fire. People scream: "Burn the books, burn the books." There is a pile of about 1,000 books written by Simon, by Rachel's brother, by other Wej authors, by Communist authors, and anyone who had written critiques of the Sizan Party.

Teacher Tip ✔

Choose a Nergman character and then a Wejish character.

Card 7A (Ulf)

"Burn the books! Burn the books written by Un-Nergman authors!"

Card 7B (Dirk)

"Let us throw these Wejish books into the flames!"

Choice Moment 1 (Thomas)

You see these books burning. What do you do?

Choice Moment 2 (Dr. Stephen)

You see these books burning. What do you do?

Choice Moment 3 (Simon and Rachel)

You see your own books and your family's books being burned. What do you do?

Choice Moment 4 (Dirk, Erhard, and Arnold)

You are police officers. How do you react to this scene? What do you do?

Teacher Tip

Go one by one through the characters to get their actions until some conflict starts to arise. Have those characters interact with each other. Perhaps a Wejish character tries to take books away. What do the Nergman officers do? What if an officer pressures Nergmans to participate?

Card 7C (A Nergman in the Crowd)

Find a Wej and hand him or her a book. Yell out: "Throw in some books. Show that you're with us."

Choice Moment 5 (Wej)

You are given a book to throw. What do you do?

Teacher Tip

Don't forget to pause, lay out the stakes, and get feedback, insight, and suggestions from observers.

Scene 2: The Boycott

Role-Players

- Police officers: Dirk, Erhard, Arnold.
- Store owners: Robert, Michael, Dolf, Kurt/Marina.
- Shoppers: Rupert, Werner, Manfred, Hannah, Therese, Sandra, Gabriella, Sophia, Leopold.

Set-up

Move three desks together and ask the store owners to make a sign for their store.

Teacher Tip

Make copies of the chart to hand one to each shopper so (s)he knows what to purchase and where.

Table 5.6 Shopping List for Boycott Role-Play

Shopper	Item to Purchase	Store Where you Normally Shop
Rupert	Carrots and Potatoes	Dolf's grocery
Werner	Chicken Legs	Robert's butcher shop
Manfred	Bread	Michael's grocery
Hannah	Cereal	Dolf's grocery
Therese	Bread	Kurt and Marina's bakery
Sandra	Goose	Robert's butcher shop
Gabriella	Bread	Michael's grocery
Sophia	Apples and Pears	Michael's grocery
Leopold	Onions and Garlic	Dolf's grocery

Teacher Reads

Erhard, Arnold, and Dirk stand outside Michael's grocery store. The store to the right is another grocery owned by Dolf and then a butcher shop owned by Robert, a Wejish businessman. They've all known each other for years. They are competitors, but they also help each other out once in awhile. Other Nergmans and Wejs are doing their afternoon shopping.

Two Sizan officers stand outside Robert and Michael's doors.

Card 7D (Sizan Officers)

Your Orders:
You have received orders from the national government that today is a full boycott of all Wej stores. You are under strict orders to not allow any shoppers into Wej-owned businesses and to arrest anyone who disobeys.

Choice Moment 6 (Shoppers)

Many of you normally shop at Michael and Robert's store. What do you do?

Choice Moment 7 (Police Officers)

How do you respond to the shoppers?

Choice Moment 8 (Dolf)

How do you respond to this scene? What do you do?

Choice Moment 9 (Other Characters)

How do you respond to this scene? What do you do?

Teacher Reads

That afternoon, the characters are walking home and they see signs on the wall: "Law: Only Nergmans are allowed to hold government positions."

Purchasing Chart

Note: Additional purchasing charts are available online at:
http://davidsherrin.wix.com/davidsherrin

Weimar and Nazi Germany 8: Schools and Family

The Gist: This lesson explores Nazi rule in Germany during the mid-1930s, as the web of discrimination continues to tighten in all areas of public life. To prepare for the role-play continue to assign some students life-changes, such as marriages, divorces, new jobs, injuries, children, etc.

Homework #7: Schools and Families

Compelling Question: How hopeful do you feel about relations between Nergmans and Wejs in Nergmay?

Source	Title or Author
A.	NSDAP Mass Rally at the *Sportpalast* in Berlin (August 15, 1935)[32]
B.	"For Aryans Only": Official Inscription on Park Benches (1935)[33]
C.	*The Eternal Jew* [*Der ewige Jude*], Film Poster (September 1940)[34]
D.	Gershom Scholem on the Atmosphere in Munich in the Early 1920s (Retrospective Account, 1977)[35]
Extension	Zeller, pp. 82–91.

Warm-up
Option 1: Take six minutes to begin to read the sources for tonight's homework and identify one point you would make in a café conversation about life in Nergmay.

Option 2: Write a paragraph reflection from your character. How does the character feel about his or her actions so far? Why is (s)he making those decisions?

Option 3: Write one paragraph about your experience role-playing. To what extent has it helped your learning (or not)? How does it compare to other ways of learning history?

Background

Nergmay is a different place. The atmosphere is tense, like a town awaiting a hurricane. The nation seems infected with fear, a fear that is beginning to affect all interactions.

Sizan newspapers begin urging readers to be on the lookout for Wejs and report any of their failures or shortcomings.

Judges grant permission to two men to divorce their wives because the women are Wejish, reasoning that such marriages would yield mixed offspring that would only weaken the Nergman race.

You often encounter squads of uniformed young people marching and singing. Banners with the red, white, and black insignia of the Sizan Party are hanging from balconies.

A recent law states that no Wejs are allowed to work in government offices any longer.

Things have changed in schools. The Terhil Salute starts everyday. Everyone is expected to salute. Shopkeepers salute customers. The teachers no longer say "Good morning"—they say "Praise Terhil." But the Wejish kids aren't allowed to say "Praise Terhil."

An American consular official, watching the changing scene in Nergmay, writes that the situation of the Wejs in Nergmay is growing more and more difficult. Neighbors begin to look at each other, to watch each other. They even search each other's ancestry. It is through this that Wilma learns that her father was actually born as a Wej. To the Nergmans that makes her a Wej too.

For strong performance in the previous role-play in taking on their persona and/or achieving success, the following characters may choose to achieve one personal goal (such as marriage): _____.

For completing the homework and/or debriefing it, the following characters earn +2 points for intelligence: _____.

All Nergmans may choose any characteristic and add +1 points: _____.

Scene 1: The School's Faculty Room

Role-Players
- Police officers: Erhard, Dirk, Arnold.
- Teachers: Katharina, Therese, Rachel.

Teacher Reads

During the faculty lunch break, toward the end of the school year, three of the teachers are quietly sipping coffee and eating their lunch. They are talking about some of their recent lessons. Suddenly, a few police officers open the door and enter the faculty lunchroom.

Card 8A (Officer)

"Praise Terhil! Teachers, Wejish children are no longer allowed in our schools. You must go to your classes and tell the Wej children to go home."

Choice Moment 1 (Teachers)

The police officers have demanded that you expel your Wejish students. What do you do?

Teacher Tip

If the teachers refuse, you could be the principal and insist that they have to do it or they will be fired. If they continue to refuse, fire them and then go into the classroom and expel the Wejish students. If they agree, have them go and speak to the class and expel the students. The students can finish the day but they cannot return tomorrow.

Scene 2: The Classroom

Role-Players
- Teachers: Katharina, Therese, Rachel (depending on the previous scene).
- NPC: Choose four students to play second-grade children. Two should be Nergman and two should be Wejish.

Teacher Reads

Towards the end of the day, the teachers decide it is time to have a conversation with their students. Depending on their desires, they either speak to the whole class or pull the Wejish students aside. It is time to tell them about the new change in educational policy.

Choice Moment 2 (Teachers)

How do you explain the situation to the students, especially to the Wejish students?

Choice Moment 3 (Students)

How do you respond to the teachers' statements? What questions do you ask?

Teacher Tip

It sometimes takes a try or two to get something genuine from the students. This process can involve pauses and discussion that includes the observing students. In one class, the student was unrealistically aggressive toward the teacher. In another, the student didn't seem to care and said "fine." We paused to discuss the stakes of the moment and we got advice on reactions from the observers, which led to a stronger role-play.

Scene 3: The Home

Role-Players:
- The previous students (Wejish and Nergman).
- Two to four characters who are parents, including Wejs and Nergmans.

Teacher Reads

The students, Wejish and Nergman, are walking home together. Some of the Wejish students are crying.

Choice Moment 4 (Nergman Students)

How do you respond to them?

Teacher Reads

They arrive at their homes where their parents are sitting outside, drinking lemonade and chatting, waiting for them, as they always do. The Nergman and Wejish children are neighbors. The Wejish children walk in with their heads down. It looks like they are hiding something. But then one speaks.

Card 8B (Wejish Child)

Action: You are crying.
"Mom, they kicked me and all the other Wejish students out of school today. I was so embarrassed. What happened? What did I do wrong?"

Card 8C (Nergman Child)

"Mom, the Wejish students got kicked out of school today. Why did that happen? Was that the right thing?"

Teacher Tip ✔

For this scene, I like to have students either in small groups (multiple discussions happening at the same time) or fishbowls, going one at a time. Afterwards we can debrief the various discussions. Pair up all the parents with their children. Give them all one or two minutes to explain to their children what is happening. It is helpful to push the "children" to ask questions of their parents. You may start to see emotion from some of the role-players, especially the parents, as they put themselves in this situation. One time, I pulled a child over and prompted her to ask "Why aren't we good enough to learn with the other kids." The "parents" just melted. As parents shifted between telling the hard truth and glossing over the situation, we paused to debate as a larger class whether eight-year-olds should be told the truth about things like hate and discrimination.

Scene 4: The Kitchen (Optional)

Teacher Reads

The next day, no Wejish students come to school. Meanwhile, many intermarried couples have begun to question what to do about their relationships. Is it best, in this new Nergmay, to stick together or to separate from each other?

Role-Players (depending on the make-up of the class and the relationships you may need to shift these pairs)

- Katharina and Stephen.
- Sandra and Robert.
- Dolf and Marisa.

Teacher Tip

What do Wej and Nergman couples do? Make them have this conversation. You may use the following cards to help them start.

Card 8D (Robert)

"Honey, it is hard now for Wejs and Nergmans to be together. Will you stay with me?"

Choice Moment 5 (Sandra)

What do you do? Do you stay with your Wejish husband?

Card 8E (Marisa)

"Dolf, it is dangerous for me to be a Wej. We have been dating a long time. Can we get married? It might protect me."

Choice Moment 6 (Dolf)

Will you marry a Wej?

Card 8F (Katharina)

"Honey, it is dangerous for you to be a Wej. Why don't you convert to be Tiashcrin like me? It may keep you safe.

Choice Moment 7 (Stephen)

What do you do? Do you convert?

Weimar and Nazi Germany 9: Propaganda and Hitler Youth

The Gist: This role-play examines the role of propaganda and education in Nazi Germany, especially regarding youngsters. How did the Nazis disseminate their message and how did they get people to join their party?

Homework #8: Solutions

Compelling Question: What do you think members of your community (Nergmans or Wejs) should do to address the current situation/problems?

A Special Assignment

The Basic Assignment for Wejs: With growing persecution of the Wejish people in Nergmay, community leaders such as Dr. Stephen have called for individuals to come to a Wejish Community Board meeting to discuss their options and decide on next steps. Wejs must bring proposals of what they should do and why.

Write one or two paragraphs as a **proposal** from your character's perspective. What are the problems that Wejs are facing and what should the community do as a solution?

The Basic Assignment for Nergmans: There is a meeting at the city hall at which only Nergmans are invited. You have received orders to do something on the night of November 8 to make the Wejs feel more unwelcome in Nergmay. The local government has sought to receive input from its citizens. What can you do to make the Wejs feel more unwanted in Nergmay?

Write one or two paragraphs as a **proposal** from your character's perspective. What should the Nergmans do to make the Wejs feel more unwelcome in Nergmay?

- Julius: Write a one-page newspaper editorial for *The Thunderstorm* giving your opinion.

- Marina: The editor of the *The Thunderstorm* has asked you to make two propaganda illustrations explaining what the Nergmans should do. Make those illustrations.

Source	Title or Author
A.	The Aryan Family (undated)[36]
B.	Youth League Camp Site (1933)[37]
C.	Young Girls Post a Notice Advertising the League of German Girls (1934)[38]
D.	Members of the Hamburg *Jungvolk* are Instructed in the Use of Carbine Rifles at a Hitler Youth Camp on the Baltic Sea (1938)[39]
Extension	Zeller, pp. 92–96.

Warm-up

What do you think would happen if a German protested Nazi policies? Why?

Background

One of the most popular activities for children during this time is to be in the Terhil Youth. More than half of all Nergman children are in the Terhil Youth. The organization was divided into two categories, one for members aged 10–14 and the other for those aged 14–18. The structure was based on a military model, with squads, platoons, and companies.

The focus, especially for boys, is on military training in preparation for becoming a soldier at 18. Parades, speeches, and camp gatherings are often on the calendar. The goal of girls was to prepare for motherhood and learn to raise children who would be educated in the ways of Terhil and the Sizans. They were indoctrinated with "racial pride" and told to avoid any contact with Wejs.

The Terhil Youth are told they will be the future "supermen" of Nergmay and the next leaders of the Sizan government. Wejs are not allowed in the Terhil Youth.

Wejs are no longer allowed to teach at Nergman schools. They see a sign on the street: only Nergmans are allowed to attend schools and universities. A few months later, the following law is published: Wejs are not allowed to be citizens of Nergmany. Wejs may not marry Nergmans, or have sexual relations with Nergmans. Wejs may not hire Nergman women to work in their homes. Wejs may not display the Nergman flag.

For strong performance in the previous role-play in taking on their persona and/or achieving success, the following Nergman characters may choose one new skill: _____.

For completing the homework and/or debriefing it, the following characters earn +1 point for force: _____.

Scene 1: The Movie Theater

Role-Players
Everyone.

Scenery
Turn off the lights; show an image of 1938 film *The Adventures of Robin Hood* on the projector. Make sure you have downloaded (or have Internet access) the YouTube clip called "The Eternal Jew."

Teacher Reads
It is a Saturday afternoon. With such difficult times in Nergmay, you decide you need a break. You see a poster for the new movie *The Adventures of Robin Hood* starring Errol Flynn. Everyone is talking about it and so you head to the movie theater to see it. You're so thrilled just to relax. Many of you are with your spouses and children. You settle into the theater, sit in your seat, and begin to munch on popcorn. As the movie is about to begin, the manager of the theater makes an announcement. "Ladies and gentlemen, my apology. The film *Robin Hood* has not arrived yet. However, we are delighted to show you a Nergman classic, the recent movie *The Eternal Wej*. We hope you enjoy."

Teacher Tip

Pause to hear the characters' thoughts and emotions. Does anyone do anything? Begin the film. Stop at one or two points (and step out of character) during the four minutes to check for understanding about the film's comparison of Jews to the plague and to rats as well as the use of language. Provide the students with one or two choice moments to "do something" if they choose.

Scene 2: The Park

Role-Players
- Kurt, Marina, and child (NPC).
- One other Nergman couple and child (NPC).
- Ulf and/or Rupert.

Teacher Reads

It is Sunday afternoon, one of those lovely days in early spring when it is just warm enough not to wear a jacket but before the harsh sun of the summer. A few Nergman friends have gathered with their children for lemonade and cakes in the park. You are sitting on blankets, watching the kids kick a soccer ball around. You smile as a cloud passes away and the sun's rays shine directly on the children's laughing faces. They run over to you, sitting down next to you as they breathe heavily from the sport.

Card 9A (Kurt and Marina's Child)

"Mom and Dad, I decided I want to sign up to be in the Terhil Youth. A bunch of my friends are joining and it looks like so much fun! Can I go join after school today?"

Choice Moment 1 (Kurt and Marina)

What do you do? What are the advantages and disadvantages of allowing the child to become a member of the Terhil Youth?

Teacher Tip

Before or after the parents give their decision, it is worthwhile to discuss as a class the implications of this decision for them and their children. What values should they consider? Is it more important for them to keep their children safe or to push them to "do the right thing?"

Card 9B (Nergman Child)

"Dad, my friends are all joining the Terhil Youth and they say that I should join to learn how to fight the Wejs. Is that okay?"

Choice Moment 2 (Nergman Parents)

What do you do? What are the advantages and disadvantages of allowing the child to become a member of the Terhil Youth?

Teacher Tip ✔

In the same vein, it is useful to debrief this situation and the ways in which this child's motivation differed from the first. Does it matter if one is going for the fun and the other to persecute Wejs?

Scene 3: In the Plaza

Role-players
- Sandra, Gabriella, Leopold, Barib Joshua.
- Six students as Nergman youth (NPCs).
- Two students as Wej youth (NPCs).

Teacher Reads

It is a week later. You're all on the street in one of the main plazas of Lerbin. The leaves are changing colors. It would be really nice out—except for what you know is going on around you. Those of you who are Nergman are sitting at a café, having coffee. The officers are patrolling the streets. Those of you who are Wejs are walking home from Kurt's store, with your children and the few groceries you can afford. Other Nergmans are sitting at the café, sipping a coffee.

A group of eight Terhil Youth, dressed in their uniforms, are coming home from a meeting. Those of you who have children in the Terhil Youth are there.

They are handing out pamphlets "Eat Wejish Food and You'll Die" and "The Wejs are our misfortune." They see the families of Wejs walking down the street.

Before anyone can realize, they have circled around them.

Card 9C (Nergman Youth)

Shout: "Wej Ikey, nose spikey."

Teacher Reads

They move closer, laughing at the Wejs, pointing at their patches on the clothing. They start to get angry.

Card 9D (Nergman Youth)

Shout: "Wej pig."

Teacher Reads

One of them shouts "Wej pig" at Rachel's child. Another one moves closer to Sandra and Rachel's child. No one is smiling. Everyone in the plaza is staring. The police are nearby. They are the only ones laughing. Rachel's youngest daughter, only eight years old, starts to whimper in fear.

Choice Moment 3 (Everyone)

What do the Wej parents do? What do the Nergman parents do? What do the Nergman and Wej youth do?

Weimar and Nazi Germany 10: Communal Choices PDD

The Gist: The central idea of this PDD is for students to explore the difficult choices that individuals and communities must make during times of crisis. This PDD involves decisions that were made as the Nazi Party's power grew in Germany.

Homework #9: Communal Choices

Compelling Question: How hopeful do you feel about your future?

Source	Title or Author
A.	*Jew Süß [Jud Süß]*, Film Still (1940)[40]
B.	Viennese Jews are Forced to Scour the Streets (March/April 1938)[41]
C.	Decree from the Head of the Security Police to the Heads of all State Police Offices (September 3, 1939)[42]
D.	Josef Meisinger on "Combating Homosexuality as a Political Task" (April 5–6, 1937)[43]
Extension	Weissmann Klein, pp. 28–33, 82–89.

Warm-up

Option 1: Prepare for the PDD (See format below).

Option 2: What do you think are three important factors that influence why people make their decisions in Nergmay?

Teacher Tip

I run this role-play as two separate PDDs and then a follow-up event (*Kristallnacht*). I choose to have the Wejish community deliberate first and then the Nergmans. We do these role-plays in a fishbowl format, which allows the other students to be active observers. Regardless of decisions that are made, it will take time to implement them, which allows for a *Kristallnacht* role-play to follow. If you have an ICT class with a special education teacher, it is valuable to take one of the groups out of the room to hold two completely separate PDDs so each group does not know what the other has decided.

Background

Five years have passed since the Sizan Party took control. Nergmay is not the same place it was when you were kids. Lerbin is in a state of fear. The Sizan guards and troops seem to be all over. A cold wind sweeps through the city streets. Often, the streets are empty. Nergmay is now in the midst of a war with other neighboring countries, ever since Terhil broke the treaty and entered a demilitarized zone.

Due to the recent laws, Wejs have lost their jobs and have been kicked out of school. Their children had to be put in Wejish schools instead of public schools. Books written by Wejs were burned on the streets. Wejish stores have been boycotted. Perhaps most threatening, Sizan soldiers and Nergman children march, chanting "When Wej-blood squirts from the knife—things go well for us."

In July, a few months ago, a sign went up on the walls of public buildings: Wejs must apply for and carry identification cards. Wejish doctors may not practice medicine. Rachel has lost her job. Stephen has been forced to stop practicing medicine. Simon, a distinguished professor of history, has been fired. Many begin to turn to Barib Joshua, their religious leader, for guidance during this time. Others turn away from anything having to do with their religion. Many, who previously had believed that they were more Nergman than Wejish, begin to wonder why the rest of the world doesn't see them that way.

For strong performance in the previous role-play in taking on their persona and/or achieving success, the following characters may choose one new possession: _____.

For completing the homework and/or debriefing it, the following characters earn +1 point for dexterity: _____.

All Nergmans may choose any characteristic and add +2 points: _____.

PDD 1: The Wejish Community Board

Teacher Reads

With growing persecution of the Wejish people in Nergmay, community leaders such as Dr. Stephen have called for individuals to come to a Wejish Community Board meeting to discuss their options and decide on next steps. Wejs must bring proposals of what they should do and why. Dr. Stephen will open the meeting with a brief welcome, then people will be invited up to give formal proposals. Following this, there will be an open debate for 5–10 minutes. Finally, the members of the Board will vote on the official policy and strategy of the Wejish community. The question in front of you: What should your community do about the growing persecution of Wejs in Nergmay?

Card 10A (Dr. Stephen)

Ladies and gentlemen, my brothers and sisters, my fellow Wejs. This is a difficult time for all of us. We are under attack here in Nergmay not just by our neighbors but by the government itself. We need to discuss our options, to hear our options, and to come up with a plan. We, the members of the Board, will hear you out carefully. We will then make a decision about the official plan of the Wejish community. We now invite you up to hear your proposals.

Format of PDD

1. Dr. Stephen's welcome (Card 10A).
2. Official reading of proposals and speeches.
3. Open discussion.
4. Decision (by vote) of the Council.

Teacher Tip

After students have a chance to give their proposals, I ask Dr. Stephen or whoever is on the board to restate the main proposals. In my class, students suggested that they could boycott Nergman stores in retaliation, try to leave Nergmay, or start a revolution. Once he had summarized those points, they then entered into a debate on the pros and cons of those proposals, including the level of danger they might face. He chose, in the end, for the community to support the emigration of Wejs. We debriefed with "Why is this decision hard to make?"

PDD 2: A Nergman Meeting

Teacher Reads

Life is changing rapidly in Nergmay. There is a meeting at the city hall at which only Nergmans are invited. You have received orders to do something on the night of November 8 to make the Wejs feel more unwelcome in Nergmay. The local government has sought to receive input from its citizens. What can you do to make the Wejs feel more unwanted in Nergmay? Present your plans, debate them, and then Deputy Ulf will make the final decision.

Card 10B (Deputy Ulf)

Ladies and gentlemen, fellow Nergmans. This is a difficult time in which Wejs continue to attack the Nergman people. We must respond. We know that Wejs have been a disease in our midst for generations. The national government has sent a request to us for an action to make Wejs feel unwelcome here, a nationwide action on November 8. We must decide what to do here in our city of Lerbin. Your ideas are welcome and then at the end of the evening I will make a decision.

Format of PDD

1. Deputy Ulf's welcome (Card 10B).
2. Official reading of proposals and speeches.
3. Open discussion.
4. Decision (by vote) of the Council.

Teacher Tip

Ulf should summarize the main points and proposals before entering into step 3 (open discussion). In my class, characters suggested breaking into homes and steal valuable items, arson, kicking them out of the cities, and giving them the choice to leave or they would die. Other classes have proposed taking the Wejish leader hostage to convince him to urge his people to leave. The first two options are, of course, strong entrance points into *Kristallnacht*.

Weimar and Nazi Germany 11:
The Night of Broken Glass

The Gist: This role-play is meant to introduce students to the shocking and transformational event of *Kristallnacht*. The impact of this evening was tremendous on the psyche of all people living in Germany. One former Hitler Youth member, Alfons Heck, explained that after *Kristallnacht* no one could honestly say that they did not know what was taking place toward the Jews. I do not use a separate background reading because this scene takes place soon after the previous communal discussions.

Homework #10: The Night of Broken Glass

Compelling Question: What should you and your people do after the Night of Broken Glass? What does it tell you about life in Nergmay?

Source	Title or Author
A.	*Kristallnacht* Order (November 10, 1938)[44]
B.	The Morning after the Night of Broken Glass [*Kristallnacht*] in Kassel: The Looted and Destroyed Jewish Community House (November 10, 1938)[45]
C.	The Morning after the Night of Broken Glass [*Kristallnacht*] in Berlin: Shattered Shop Windows (November 10, 1938)[46]
D.	American Consul Samuel Honaker's Description of Anti-Semitic Persecution and *Kristallnacht* and its Aftereffects in the Stuttgart Region (November 12 and November 15, 1938)[47]
Extension	Zeller, pp. 131–46.

Warm-up
Option 1: What choices do individual Nergmans and Wejs have in Nergmay? Do they have the choice to resist?

Option 2: Take six minutes and read Source A from tonight's homework. Based on the reading, what do you think will happen in the role-play?

THUNDERSTORM

Lerbin| Nergmay | Seltsam

SURPRISE FEATURE

Movie goers earlier this week had a surprise. Due to a slight error in the theater not carrying the film, Robin Hood the movie theater instead started showing the film: The Forever Wej. This wonderful film about the Wejish race documents their history. For the protection of the audience police officers ensured the exit would be safe... (Pg. 3)

LERBIN FOR NERGMANS

November 8th is the deadline for the decision for which we must act to deal with the Wejish problem. In the middle of the meeting a disruptive painter (Zeeter) made many anti Sizan arguments raising questions on how pure his blood was... (Pg. 2)

LERBIN'S FINEST

Earlier this week a struggle outside some stores turned deadly when police officer Arnold shot and killed an asawhile attempting to get past Arnold and two other officers. Police sergeant Dirk was also there and had this to say, "The... (Pg. 12)

THE TWILIGHT OF SHATTERED GLASS

Earlier this week many of Lerbin's citizens observed and participated in a wide spread protest against the Wej. The primary guidelines were that Wejish shops be destroyed but not looted. A second priority was to purify Wejish buildings. On a closer to home level the police took the Wejish leader into custody as was discussed in the previous town meeting. During the protests some individual events came to light causing doubts among the police and the general populous to start, questioning even our own neighbors motives. A letter was dispatched from the central government telling the police to inform local government officials about the protests and to enforce strict laws to keep the general populous from getting swept away in violence. Despite the heavy police presence some rowdy store owners attacked protesters. At least one was killed in self defense by the

police when he came out wielding knives ready to attack the protesters. Two individuals known about the town also stuck out for their actions that night. One I cannot talk about too much due to an ongoing investigation.

However a starting investigation carried out on one police sergeant Arnold has turned up some interesting facts about his past pro Wej tendencies. This investigation was started when it came to the attention of the other officers that Arnold was the only one not on duty at the time of the protests when he should have. After some further investigation it was revealed that he has had some long standing affiliations with Wejes. For a time before he was a police officer he worked for a Wejish store owner. And we even recently learned that he had been married to a Wej and had Wejish children. Now due to the sensitive nature of this event the police have not yet released any final statements on what is going to happen. And the other investigation is still under way. But now the police has started asking that if anyone knows anything about people who may have lied about their race to report.

LERBIN MEETS OVER WEJ PROBLEM

In Lerbin today our great city will be deciding on what exactly to do about the Wejish problem. Through the Sizan party many cities in Nergmany have been calling councils to declare how to deal with the Wejish problem in more and more extreme ways. This meeting specifically is to come up with new ways to make the Wejish community feel less welcome. No Wejs will be allowed to attend this meeting. This is to prevent conflicts of interests corrupting the ideas and voting. At the same time the Wejs have called a meeting of their own to conspire whatever they have you. However most of the attention is focused on the main meeting of Nergmans. This meeting, I feel, will be the one that will set the path for Lerbin in years to come. So a careful and well thought out decision must be reached. One that keeps in mind what is best for the people of our great city. For many generations the Wejs have plagued our lands. And now with the Sizan party we have a chance to change this. But with this new found power no rash decisions should be made. It is both dangerous to over react and under react. For no matter what happens there are bad Nergmans and good Wejs...(Pg. 4)

Figure 5.3 Darren's Night of Broken Glass homework. Note how Darren, who played Julius, took advantage of his role as the journalist in his homework assignments.

Note for Teachers

We make a list of options for the characters based on the warm-up. Most often, students come up with at least four: fleeing, hiding, or fighting back. I might add in a couple more: sending your children away on the child transport (which I briefly explain) or waiting. The important move to set-up the next few days is to make clear that all individuals must make a choice of a course of action. If they want to hide, for instance, then they need to find a Nergman (after class) who will agree to hide them. But they need to be careful and to keep it secret (but to tell me). I remind them there are spies. They need to have a plan of where to hide. If they want to fight back, they need a plan.

I take one day off from role-playing after this lesson to introduce the unit assessment, during which I can meet with all Wejs to record their choices on the chart below. We go over the details of their plans so that I can include them in my subsequent scenes. For example, one year 1–2 characters might decide to assassinate Terhil, but this year they chose to kill the Sizan leader in class (Rupert). They decided to invite him to a dinner in his honor and then to stab him. I included that instead of one of the other planned scenes the following day. Here, you may also have students begin to forge documents for each other, to hide each other, etc. Hopefully some students will tell you this in secret so you can arrange accordingly.

Table 5.8 Examples of Character Choices for Resistance

Option	Students who Choose this Option
1. Try to escape the country to the United States.	
2. Try to pretend to be Nergman and hide in disguise.	
3. Try to find a Nergman to hide you.	
4. Try to send your child on child transport out of the country to be taken care of by someone in Great Britain.	
5. Try to fight back or to assassinate a leader.	

Scene 1: Streets and Homes

Role-Players
- At home: Kurt, Marina, Dolf, Marisa, Simon, Sophia, Joshua, Gabriella.
- On the streets: Ulf, Dirk, Erhard, Rupert, Thomas.

Background

It is very soon after the communal meetings about the future of Nergmay. It is around 1.20am on November 10. The night before, a Wej radical whose parents had been expelled from their homes shot and killed a Nergman official in Paris. The news shocked all Nergmay and unsettled many. Most of you are sleeping comfortably under your warm blankets. You dig in deep under the covers to protect against the chill of the autumn night. You awaken, startled, at a sound.

Teacher Tip

The sensory experience in this role-play is important. I make sure to turn off the lights and to prepare the sound of broken glass, which I use repeatedly and randomly throughout the scenes. You can locate a sound-clip online.[48]

You hear it again.

Card 11A (Sophia speaking to Simon)

"I think that is the sound of breaking glass across the street."

Choice Moment 1 (Simon)

What do you do?

Teacher Tip

Run through the reactions of the characters at home to get a sense of their first response.

Teacher Reads

Those who walk to the window see a frightful sight outside. Groups of men, some in uniform and some in civilian clothes, are armed with sledgehammers and axes. You can tell from looking around that they have targeted Wejish homes and Wejish stores. You see two Wejish homes with their windows broken. You see the store of a Wejish tailor that has been destroyed.

Card 11B (Erhard, Dolf, Ulf, Arnold)

You have received the following orders from the head of the national Sizan Security Police:

- Gather loyal soldiers and civilians.
- Wear civilian clothing to pretend that tonight's action is a spontaneous uprising from the people.
- Destroy Wejish property, especially businesses and houses of worship.
- You may enter Wejish homes.
- Burn down key Wejish locations.
- Protect all non-Wejish property.
- Take prisoner wealthy Wejish men.
- You may take any means necessary to secure the above goals especially if faced with any opposition from Wejs.

You see them walk toward Robert's butcher shop and Marina's bakery.

Choice Moment 2 (Characters at Home)

What do you do?

Teacher Tip

Pause here for a discussion, reflection, and advice for the characters.

Card 11C (Gabriella)

"Joshua, I think they are heading toward our house of worship."

Choice Moment 3 (Joshua)

What do you do?

Teacher Reads
After the destruction of those shops, the Nergmans begin to walk toward the Wejish house of worship, where they gather and pray and read their holy book. Everyone knows their intentions. The streets are now filled with Nergmans. They pass by Thomas, the Nergman priest, and Rupert, the Nergman doctor, who are coming home from attending to a dying man.

Card 11D (Dirk)

"Come join us, we are destroying the Wejish homes and property!"

Choice Moment 4 (Thomas and Rupert)

What do you do?

Teacher Tip ✔

Pause to ask the observers for advice for Thomas and Rupert.

Teacher Reads

The Nergmans get to the house of worship. People all around the street watch from their windows as they approach the stained-glass windows.

Choice Moment 5 (All Characters in the Role-Play)

What do you do?

Teacher Tip

Allow the role-play to progress from here for 5–10 minutes. Each class might take it in a different direction. The seriousness of the situation has increased and dissent or resistance have more dire consequences. Afterwards, It is essential to debrief this role-play by a reflection on their choices. Additionally, the teacher should provide some additional information. With government support and organization, the troops and civilian helpers destroyed Wejish property all over the country. At least 7,500 Wejish stores were destroyed. Homes were ransacked. Some Wejs on the streets or in their homes were beaten. A total of 91 Wejs were killed, and 30,000 Wejish men disappeared. The Sizans destroyed over 1,500 houses of worship and set more than 250 of them on fire.

Teacher Reads

Soon after, signs appear on the streets: Wejs are not allowed to own any businesses or property. Wejs can be barred from the streets on certain days.

Weimar and Nazi Germany 12: Choices

Teacher Tip

I prepare a simple octagon patch that says Wej in the middle. Students must tape it to their clothing. I sometimes have them watch *The Pianist*, starting at minute 10.00, for the scene that involves the notice about the Jewish star. I ask them to reflect on the purpose of this law and their feeling in putting on the symbol.

The Gist: I find this day (or days) of role-playing to be particularly compelling because it opens up so many avenues for student choice. Usually by this point a few students playing Wejs in the role-play have begun to clamor for the option to rebel, escape, or fight back. This is their chance. We explore a few different options that Jews took in Germany to try to take their destiny into their own hands in the brief period of time between *Kristallnacht* and when the doors closed completely. We begin to grapple with the complexities of these options and their limitations.

Homework #11: Choices

Compelling Question: What should your community do? What should you do individually?

Source	Title or Author
A.	Inside of a Compulsory Identification Card for Jews, Issued in Berlin (1939)[49]
B.	The Destroyed Beer Hall after the Assassination Attempt on Hitler (November 9, 1939)[50]
C.	Siblings Hans and Sophie Scholl and Christoph Probst (left to right) of the Student Resistance Group "White Rose" (1942)[51]
D.	The Fifth Broadsheet of the "White Rose" (January 1943)[52]
Extension, Secondary Source	Fritzsche, pp. 132–42.

Teacher Tip

This role-play involves five options for Wejs to take as resistance or to secure their own survival (the survival of loved ones). This may take anywhere from one to five days depending on the choices that students have made. I often take a day off from role-playing between the last one and this one to gather and organize student choices and to make a plan. I make sure to have a filled-out copy of the chart from the previous lesson to keep track of the options and who is pursuing each one.

Warm-up
In what ways has the Sizan Party made a "them" or "other" out of the Wejs? Identify at least four ways.

Background

After the "Night of Shattered Windows," everyone knows that Nergmay will never be the same. On that night, at least 7,500 Wejish stores were destroyed. Homes were ransacked. Some Wejs on the streets or in their homes were beaten or forced to commit public humiliation. A total of 91 Wejs were killed, and 30,000 Wejish men disappeared into prisons or special camps. The Sizans destroyed over 1,500 Wejish houses of worship and set more than 250 of them on fire. They also desecrated Wejish cemeteries.

People have been spying on each other. Dirk, it turns out, had a Wej grandmother. When the government finds out, he loses his job as a police officer. Therese's mother admits to her that she was born a Wej but her parents converted her at a young age. Only Hannah and Sandra know. But will they tell?

All around you, you see signs on the walls. Signs that say "Wej" on the windows of Wejish stores. Wejs and Nergmans no longer speak to each other openly in the streets. It is too dangerous for either of them. Nergman leaders don't want the Wejs to "contaminate" them—so now Wejs can't use the swimming pools or the parks or the nice trains.

You walk down the street and you see "Wej" signs everywhere. But then you see a sign posted on the wall. All Wejs must visibly wear a patch that says "Wej" on their clothing.

For strong performance in the previous role-play in taking on their persona and/or achieving success, the following characters may choose one new skill: _____.

For completing the homework and/or debriefing it, the following characters earn +1 point for any characteristic they choose: _____.

All Wejs must sit on the floor.

Scene 1: The Nergman Emigration Office (Emigration Option)

Role-Players

- Any Wej character who previously chose to emigrate.
- One NPC playing a Nergman emigration office official.

Scenery
Sit the Nergman official behind a desk and place enough chairs in front for the Wej applicants. Hand the Nergman official the relevant document.

Teacher Tip

At the start of class I pull the student playing the Nergman official aside to go over the instruction card and the document.

Teacher Reads

Many Wejs have decided to leave Nergmay, especially after the Night of Shattered Windows. There are, however, certain steps they must take. First they must gain authorization from the Nergman Emigration Office to leave the country. A few Wejs enter the office.

Card 12A (Nergman Official)

Your instructions:

You are to allow (and even encourage) Wejs who come to your office to leave the country.

A. Ask them the following:

- What is your name, occupation, and marital status?
- Will you go alone or with family members?
- Why do you want to leave the motherland?

B. Make the following conditions very clear to them:

- Wejs who leave must agree to give up their homes and businesses to leave the country.
- Wejs must pay an emigration tax of 50 percent of their total wealth.
- They may leave their money in a Nergman bank, but can only take $4 out of the country with them.
- They must relinquish all gold and fine jewelry.
- They must sign a sheet of paper in agreement and return it by the next day.

Choice Moment 1 (Potential Emigrant)

How do you respond to the conditions? Do you continue with your plan?

Teacher Tip

This is an excellent moment for a pause to discuss the options and hear advice from observers. Why is this a difficult decision?

Scene 2: The American Consulate (Emigration Option)

Teacher Tip

The annual quota for all Nergmans (including Wejs) that the United States is accepting this year is 25,957, but the main obstacle was a 1930 U.S. State Department Regulation that required consular officials abroad to adopt a new interpretation of regulations barring prospective immigrants that were likely to become public charges. In other words, if they would not find work, they were not permitted to receive a visa.[53]

I call over a student who will play the NPC consular officer to go over the forms and the process.

Teacher Reads

The process of leaving does not just involve getting permission from Nergmay. You need to find a country to go to, which will accept Wej refugees. Your neighboring countries are cut off because of the war. You have chosen the United States, but it has a limit of 25,957 people who can come from Nergmay each year and so many want to leave. You need to secure an entrance visa. You arrive at the United States consulate in Lerbin. You walk nervously into the room. The consular officer stares at you, bored and annoyed that yet another Wej is there to plead entrance into the United States. He yawns.

Card 12B (Consular Officer)

Your instructions:
You are to determine whether these Wejs would be suitable immigrants to the United States, capable of supporting themselves and contributing to the country.

A. Ask them the following questions:

- What is your name?
- What is your occupation?
- How much wealth do you have?
- Do you have a job lined up in the United States?
- What can you contribute?

- Why do you want to come to America?
- Will you be traveling with yourself or others?

B. Consider whether each Wej is a suitable immigrant based on the answers.

- You may ask them to roll a dice to see whether they have a potential sponsor in the United States. Consider a roll of 13 or higher to be sufficient.

C. Make the documentation requirements very clear to anyone who qualifies.

- Go through the cover sheet and explain the starred items.
- Show each document and what it is.
- Make clear that they actually have to fill it out and return the next day to emigrate. They must find a student outside of class who was a Wej the previous year to agree to be a sponsor.

Card 12C (Consular Officer)

"We have an application for a visa. Please fill out this form and have it signed by your bank, your doctor, and the local Nergman police office. You must also get a letter from two sponsors in the United States who are willing to vouch for you and support you if necessary."

Choice Moment 2 (Potential Immigrant)

What do you say to the consular officer?

Teacher Tip ✔

This is another strong moment for a group reflection, including advice. Depending on how this scene plays out, you may need to come back to it at the start of the next day. For example, I give applicants one day to fill out the entire application. The following day, I put them back in the consular office to check the application. Often, the character cannot leave Nergmay because it is incomplete.

All the documents for the application are available for download on my website.

Scene 3: The Child Transport

Role-Players

* Any characters who have chosen to send their kids on the trains.
* An NPC for each child of those characters.

Scenery

Set up chairs in the middle of the room for parents and children to face each other. Alternatively, you could set-up small groups with one parent–child for each one.

Teacher Tip

Pair up with parents who will send their children away with others who will role-play their children.

Teacher Reads

The child-transport program involves a series of trains that leave Nergmay to take Wej children to live with families outside the country. Many Wejs have made the difficult decision to send their children away, knowing they may never see them again. Now is the time for the parents to sit down and explain their plans to their children.

Choice Moment 3 (Parent)

What do you say to your child? How do you explain this?

Choice Moment 4 (Child)

How do you respond to your parent? What questions do you ask?

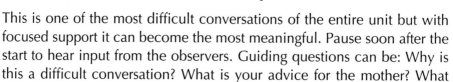

Teacher Tip

This is one of the most difficult conversations of the entire unit but with focused support it can become the most meaningful. Pause soon after the start to hear input from the observers. Guiding questions can be: Why is this a difficult conversation? What is your advice for the mother? What is your advice for the child? What are they each feeling right now?

Especially if the parent has more than one child, it can be helpful to identify the ages. This year, one parent had a child aged eight and another aged three. The older asked questions about the meaning of what was going on and why the mother wasn't joining them. The younger asked about toys and playgrounds. After, we debriefed about whether it would be harder, emotionally, to respond to the older child who understands or the younger one who doesn't?

Scene 4: The Train Office

Role-Players

- Any characters who have chosen to send their kids on the trains.
- One NPC: the organizer of the transport or Werner.

Scenery
Set up a desk facing a few chairs, which can be the train office.

Teacher Reads
Once you have had that conversation with your child, you need to go to the local organizer of the child transport to register your child. You wait on line for a bit and then have the chance to speak with the officer. Because of the war, this is the last child-transport train out of Lerbin.

Card 12D (Officer or Werner)

Can I help you?

Choice Moment 5 (Parent X)

What do you say to the officer?

Card 12E (Officer)

"I'm sorry, we've just filled up our remaining spot on this transport. We don't have plans for any future ones. I'm so sorry."

Choice Moment 6 (Parent X)

What do you do?

Teacher Tip

This is another scene in which it is essential to pause one or two times for analysis and advice. What is the mother feeling? What are her options? When considering options, think about proposing whether she should bribe the officer to get her child (or children) on the train even if this meant others would have to be struck from the list. What is the morality of such a choice? If that does happen, choose another character's child to be taken off the list. This year, "Stephen" proposed that option on his own and paid off the transport organizer. The organizer, then, had to go explain to another Wejish parent why her son was no longer on the train.

A variation on card 12E above is to tell the officer to ask how many children the mother wants to register and then to only provide space for some but not all of them. This year, for example, "Gabriella" had six children but the organizer only had room for three. This led to a lengthy class advice session in which we debated whether she could choose between her children and, if so, how to do it. After hearing the advice, Gabriella sent her middle three children.

Cameron ███

March 17, 2015

Dear diary,

I am faced with the hardest decision of my life. There is a war going on in Germany between the Jews and Germans. Being Jewish and raising my children to be strong Jews, the violence in our community with the Hitler Youth causes me to be afraid of the future. My husband and I have lost our jobs and there are rumors that the Jewish children will be banned from public schools. The Jews have been feeling very unwanted and mistreated. We're being blamed for a lot of things and many hate-acts are being committed towards us like the Germans breaking into Jew-owned stores and synagogs and ruining things. Buildings nearby are being burned to the ground, which is a scary thing to witness and is a hard thing to have to explain to your kids. Some of our family-friends have cut off all contact with everyone, and I assume they've fled the country and part of me wishes we could do the same.

I've heard about a "Child Transport" movement that takes Jewish children across the water to Great Britain to live with families there until the war is over. I'm not sure if this is a good option for my family because I don't want to be separated from my children, and at the ages of 4 and 7, it'll be very hard for them to understand. There are also a lot of things that could go wrong with this plan. I can always keep them here with us, but they'd be unsafe here.

If we choose to send them away, there's so many things that could go wrong. There's a chance I'll never see them again- if the program doesn't bring them back after the war, if something happens to them while they're traveling, or if something happens to my husband or me. At this point, I'm not sure it'll ever be safe here again, which is also a reason we should send them out of here. If they stay, they have to grow up with the Hitler Youth, who will make my kids' lives miserable. Here, they'll live in a community that acts as if we shouldn't be allowed to

Figure 5.4 Cameron's Child-Transport Homework. Keep an eye on how Cameron's "character" struggles with the emotional and ethical implication of this choice.

walk on the same sidewalk as them, use the same stores as them, or even sit on the same benches as them, as if the Jews had the plague. I'm a grown woman and I don't exactly understand why we're being treated this way. I can't imagine being a child and trying to figure out why the kids they used to be friends with, are now bullying and teasing them.

If we decide for them to go live with someone else, I'll feel like they have a safe place to live, they'll be around people who won't make them feel unwanted. Even if the chance that I'll never see them again happens, I'll know they are living in a safe community, one where there isn't a war against them. If we choose to keep them with us in Germany, we get to see them every day, I'll still continue being their mother and will be able to take care of them, which is what I love doing.

I've mentioned it to a few close friends, and most of them have said they'd send them to Great Britain because it allows them to grow in a world where they can be loved and appreciated in their community. It's way safer for a Jewish child to grow up there than in Germany at this point. My other friends have said they wouldn't dare put them on this train because of all of the risks and that they may never see them again.

I think sending them with the "Child Transport" group will give them the best chances at having a happy, successful life, even if that means running the risk of them not being apart of my life again. Sure, I'll be terribly sad, but it would be selfish of me to keep them in such a scary environment. I know there are many families facing the same decision and I hope I, as well as they, make the right decision for our children.

Sincerely,

Cameron

Figure 5.4 continued

Scene 3: Resistance

Role-Players

Any student who chooses to fight back.

Overview and Suggestions

It never occurred to me when I first started developing these role-plays that students would want to fight back. Of course, it should have. Over the years, as students began to request this more often, I started researching some examples of violent Jewish resistance in Germany (as opposed to the more well-known examples of the Warsaw Ghetto uprising or the partisans in the Belarusian forests). I require the students to come up with a plan for how they would fight back without any major weapons. Normally, their plans include either making a homemade bomb, attacking a Sizan arsenal, or assassinating Terhil (the leader). The key here is that we role-play the plan that they create.

Since each of these plots were actually attempted, their options, thus, become loosely based on the actions of Helmut Hirsch or Herbert Baum. As the facilitator of the role-play, I can allow them to do the role-play and have some limited success (killing a few Sizan officers), but ultimately I need to keep adding on enemies and obstacles until they fail. That is the history.

This year, "Leopold" and "Rachel" took a different approach. Leopold's character is a radical with a mission to upend societal injustice. Rather than assassinate Terhil, they confided in me their plan to kill "Rupert," one of the Nergman leaders of the class who had been elected to parliament. They devised a plan to invite him to dinner to honor him for his hard work. They gave him an invitation and he agreed to come. During the dinner, Leopold brought a turkey to the table and began to carve it. With an imaginary knife, he then stabbed Rupert in front of "Arnold" and "Marisa." No one else in class knew that this was going to happen. We paused to debate the ethics of killing a Sizan leader even if it would not change the larger policy. And then we debated what the rest of the characters ought to do. Arnold decided to arrest Leopold so as to not jeopardize his own scheme to leave the country.

Weimar and Nazi Germany 13:
Hiding and Deportation

The Gist: This is the final day of the role-play. The major student choices should come to some resolution during these scenes. Students should come out of this understanding the despair and fear surrounding the deportation.

Homework #12

Compelling Question: Reflect on your character's experiences and choices.

Source	Title or Author
A.	Deportation of Stuttgart Jews to Riga, Latvia—Waiting in a Detention Camp on Killesberg Hill, Stuttgart (November 1941)[54]
B.	A Resident of the Lodz Ghetto is Abused and Humiliated (1942)[55]
C.	Hungarian Jews Wait in a Clearing before being led to the Gas Chambers at Auschwitz II-Birkenau (May/June, 1944)[56]
D.	Mass Execution of Lithuanian Jews by Members of the Wehrmacht and the Lithuanian Self-Protection Unit [*Selbstschutz*] (1942)[57]
Extension, Secondary Source	Fritzsche, pp. 205–211, 234–236.

Warm-up: Role-Play Reflection

> ## Teacher Tip ✔
>
> For this last role-play you might need to wrap up some of the previous ones that were left without endings, especially those related to resistance or emigration. Any students who are in hiding must have already told you who is hiding them and where they are hiding.

Scene 1: In Hiding

Scenery

I project the following notice—"Saturday, August 29: All Wejs must report to the House of Worship on Levetzow Street with one suitcase each by 9.00 am, tomorrow morning. You will be relocated."

Teacher Reads

It is a Saturday morning. Life in Nergmay seems as if it cannot get worse for Wejs. Almost no one has jobs. The persecution and discrimination have reached all areas of life. Some of your friends and relatives have left. Food is getting scarce. You see the sign, the order, and most of you begin to pack.

Choice Moment 1 (Wejs)

What do you pack in your suitcase? Why?

Teacher Reads

The Sizan officers overseeing the relocation watch as the Wejs trudge down the streets, shoulders slumped in exhaustion and despair. They keep a careful eye out for who is following orders. They realize that the following Wejs have not reported to the house of worship for relocation: _____.

Card 13A (Sizan Officers)

Your orders:

Do whatever is necessary to find any Wejs who have not reported to the house of worship. You have full discretion should you find a Wej in hiding or escaping.

Teacher Reads

The Sizan officers storm through Lerbin searching homes for the missing Wejs. For each missing Wej, you may search two homes of your choice. If we have three hidden Wejs, for example, you may search six homes. You must decide whose home to search.

Teacher Tip

The Sizan officers have to decide whose homes to search. Have them "knock on the doors" of the homes and demand that the residents let them enter. You should know where the characters are hiding. If they choose a correct home, you may have them roll the dice to see if they locate the hidden Wejs. You also might ask the Wejs to roll to see if they make a sound, cough, etc.

Remember, everything is a choice. If the officers find Wejs they may decide what to do. This year, for example, one of the Sizan officers actually had a Wej hiding at his home, while he was searching for others. They were not able to locate the hidden characters, so I had them find other NPC characters (a mother and daughter) in hiding at an abandoned home. They decided to leave them there in secret. So then I put another NPC into the mix, a third "loyal" Sizan officer to make their response even more difficult at the next home. This year another Wej character tried to flee his hiding spot and was killed by an NPC officer. This is emotionally difficult, but needs to happen for us to come closer to mimicking reality.

Teacher Reads

From all over the city, Wejs begin to march toward their house of worship, suitcase in hands. They are stooped over, sad, frightened, but many also are hopeful, imagining that their destination cannot be worse than their recent past. They spend hours at the building until more than one thousand people are there. They are told to stand up and walk. They all do. They march over, parents, children, and spouses holding each other's hand, until they arrive at the train station. They see the trains, meant for cattle, in front of them. The officers begin to shout and push them forward. The guard dogs bark, ever more threateningly. They enter the trains, their destination and destiny unknown.

Teacher Tip

It is here that we end the role-play. I tell them that I cannot take them any further. Some years I have them read a description of the deportation found in Elie Wiesel's *Night*. The memoir *All But My Life* also has a vivid depiction. You could also ask them to journal about their thoughts, feelings, questions.

After the Role-Play

The role-play lessons take us only until the deportations. I just can't bear to go any further, into the cattle cars or through the gates of Auschwitz. Those scenes are too incomprehensible. There is still so much more of the story to tell. In these lessons, you may want to consider how you debrief the entire role-play experience, how do you teach about the concentration camps, and how you teach the post-genocidal attempts at justice.

There are myriad reflection questions you could consider for the day after the role-play ends. Here are some that I use:

- What was the point of our role-play and the study of these events leading up to the deportation?
- To what extent did characters in our role-play resist? Why?
- What do you think caused the Holocaust?
- What do you think would have been the consequence of disobedience?
- What would justice look like after this genocide?
- How did characters change during the role-play? Why?

I particularly like to follow-up on the questions 2–4 right away by looking at excerpts from Daniel Jonah Goldhagen's *Hitler's Willing Executioners*. His controversial claim was that pure anti-Semitism caused the Holocaust and that the consequences for Germans to disobey or to protest the killing of Jews were much less than we normally think.

There are so many gripping and thought-provoking resources to utilize if you spend a few days on the concentration camps. I like to give my students some heavy reading at this point, using excepts from Greda Weissmann Klein's *All But My Life*, Rudolph Hoss's *Death Dealer: The Memoirs of the SS Kommandant at Auschwitz*, and Robert Browning's *Ordinary Men*. This selection provides us with a Jewish survivor's memoir, a Nazi perpetrator's memoir, and a scholarly secondary source that tackles a few of the same questions as Goldhagen.

It is always valuable and memorable to include video and/or guest speakers. There are many videos available of survivor testimonies. Find a survivor to speak in class, the child of a survivor, or use one of the readily available online video testimonies. It is worth it. We all remember having seen a survivor speak, if we ever had the opportunity. I use the recording that I took in 2004 of my grandfather, Joseph Brandman, telling of his time along with my grandmother, Myra Brandman, in the Riga ghetto and concentration camps. I recommend taking advantage as well of the excellent array of films to choose from, whether *The Pianist, Schindler's List,* or others.

One area where I like to expand in my Holocaust studies with my students is in the realm of upstanders or the Righteous Among the Nations. The websites of Yad Vashem and Facing History and Ourselves have accessible resources on the countless heroic "ordinary" people who resisted Nazis and saved Jews.

We also spend some time putting the Holocaust in the context of the larger international political situation: World War II. This helps us move into the next piece of the puzzle: assessing the options for justice. After World War II the world had to put itself back together. Some of that was done through the creation of the United Nations. We look at the institution of the Nuremberg trials as part of that larger process of justice and restitution. Why was it created? What was its goal?

We complete this unit of study with a mock trial of Julius Streicher, which I provide in my book *Judging for Themselves.* It helps us understand and evaluate one method of justice: the international tribunal. It also helps us come to grip with the startlingly complex idea of responsibility. Who was responsible for the genocide? The soldiers who did the killings? The government officials? The propaganda artists? The ordinary citizens who turned a blind eye?

Notes

1 http://germanhistorydocs.ghi-dc.org/sub_image.cfm?image_id=3005
2 http://germanhistorydocs.ghi-dc.org/sub_image.cfm?image_id=3994
3 http://germanhistorydocs.ghi-dc.org/sub_image.cfm?image_id=4113
4 http://germanhistorydocs.ghi-dc.org/sub_image.cfm?image_id=4092
5 http://past.oxfordjournals.org/content/196/1/3.extract
6 http://antisemitism.org.il/article/82166/top-10-antisemitic-legends-and-stereotypes
7 www.icsresources.org/content/primarysourcedocs/BlackDeathAndTheJews.pdf
8 www.icsresources.org/content/primarysourcedocs/ExpulsionFromFrance.pdf
9 http://germanhistorydocs.ghi-dc.org/sub_image.cfm?image_id=3005
10 http://germanhistorydocs.ghi-dc.org/sub_image.cfm?image_id=3994
11 http://germanhistorydocs.ghi-dc.org/sub_image.cfm?image_id=4113
12 http://germanhistorydocs.ghi-dc.org/sub_image.cfm?image_id=4092
13 http://germanhistorydocs.ghi-dc.org/sub_image.cfm?image_id=4093
14 http://germanhistorydocs.ghi-dc.org/sub_image.cfm?image_id=4161
15 http://germanhistorydocs.ghi-dc.org/sub_document.cfm?document_id=3841
16 http://germanhistorydocs.ghi-dc.org/sub_image.cfm?image_id=4239
17 http://germanhistorydocs.ghi-dc.org/sub_image.cfm?image_id=4243

18 These are not the exact figures from Weimar Germany. The numbers used throughout are meant to be representative and are not the actual prices from that time and place.

19 http://germanhistorydocs.ghi-dc.org/sub_image.cfm?image_id=4102

20 www.facinghistory.org/weimar-republic-fragility-democracy/economics/homeless-mens-shelter-date-unknown-economics-1929–1933

21 www.jewishvirtuallibrary.org/jsource/Holocaust/naziprog.html

22 *Holocaust and Human Behavior.* Facing History and Ourselves, p. 147.

23 http://germanhistorydocs.ghi-dc.org/sub_document.cfm?document_id=3845

24 http://germanhistorydocs.ghi-dc.org/print_document.cfm?document_id=1891

25 http://germanhistorydocs.ghi-dc.org/print_document.cfm?document_id=1982

26 http://germanhistorydocs.ghi-dc.org/sub_document.cfm?document_id=2325

27 http://germanhistorydocs.ghi-dc.org/sub_document.cfm?document_id=1520

28 http://germanhistorydocs.ghi-dc.org/sub_image.cfm?image_id=2198

29 http://germanhistorydocs.ghi-dc.org/print_document.cfm?document_id=2070

30 http://germanhistorydocs.ghi-dc.org/sub_document.cfm?document_id=1505

31 http://germanhistorydocs.ghi-dc.org/sub_document.cfm?document_id=1519

32 http://germanhistorydocs.ghi-dc.org/sub_image.cfm?image_id=1901

33 http://germanhistorydocs.ghi-dc.org/sub_image.cfm?image_id=2090

34 http://germanhistorydocs.ghi-dc.org/sub_image.cfm?image_id=2331

35 http://germanhistorydocs.ghi-dc.org/sub_document.cfm?document_id=3911

36 http://germanhistorydocs.ghi-dc.org/sub_image.cfm?image_id=2040

37 http://germanhistorydocs.ghi-dc.org/sub_image.cfm?image_id=2054

38 http://germanhistorydocs.ghi-dc.org/sub_image.cfm?image_id=2056

39 http://germanhistorydocs.ghi-dc.org/sub_image.cfm?image_id=2055

40 http://germanhistorydocs.ghi-dc.org/sub_image.cfm?image_id=2332

41 http://germanhistorydocs.ghi-dc.org/sub_image.cfm?image_id=1990

42 http://germanhistorydocs.ghi-dc.org/sub_document.cfm?document_id=1509

43 http://germanhistorydocs.ghi-dc.org/sub_document.cfm?document_id=1558

44 www.jewishvirtuallibrary.org/jsource/Holocaust/kristallnacht_order.html

45 http://germanhistorydocs.ghi-dc.org/sub_image.cfm?image_id=1952

46 http://germanhistorydocs.ghi-dc.org/sub_image.cfm?image_id=1956

47 http://germanhistorydocs.ghi-dc.org/docpage.cfm?docpage_id=2351

48 shockwave.com or soundbible.com

49 http://germanhistorydocs.ghi-dc.org/sub_image.cfm?image_id=1966

50 http://germanhistorydocs.ghi-dc.org/sub_image.cfm?image_id=1931

51 http://germanhistorydocs.ghi-dc.org/sub_image.cfm?image_id=2197

52 http://germanhistorydocs.ghi-dc.org/sub_document.cfm?document_id=1515

53 www.ushmm.org/museum/exhibit/online/stlouis/teach/supread.htm
www.pbs.org/wgbh/amex/holocaust/filmmore/reference/primary/barmemo.html

54 http://germanhistorydocs.ghi-dc.org/sub_image.cfm?image_id=2870

55 http://germanhistorydocs.ghi-dc.org/sub_image.cfm?image_id=1971

56 http://germanhistorydocs.ghi-dc.org/sub_image.cfm?image_id=1979

57 http://germanhistorydocs.ghi-dc.org/sub_image.cfm?image_id=1973

Examples of Literature Role-Plays

6 *Fences, The Pearl,* and More

The role-play for this book *The Pearl,* made me think of literature in some new ways. Like how to truly get in the characters' shoes. Role-playing gets you to discuss books in better ways because as you're role-playing you have to think of what your character would do forcing you deeper into the mind of the author and his/her intent. It also helps me understand the book better. I do like this, because I enjoy going deeper into the context, and I like actually feeling like the character.

(Andrew, 11th-grader)

I loved role-playing as a way of learning b/c as a reader while you read you are suppose to imagine how scene is while reading. Role-playing helps me imagine and better understand what is going on in the book. I also noticed that actually participating in the role-play as a character helps you know how the character is feeling.

(Mamadou, 11th grader)

Figure 6.1 Students in Literature Role-Play of *A View from the Bridge*

The first three chapters of this book set-up how to create and execute role-plays, including those based on works of literature. As I explained earlier, students who role-play literature come out with an unforgettable experience and a deeper understanding, especially, of themes like character and conflict.

Since those strategies can be used for countless novels and plays, and it is easier to create a new role-play in English than in social studies, it is not necessary to provide such in-depth ready-to-go units. However, in the following pages I provide some model scripts for how literature role-plays may look in action in the classroom. I connect what we are saying and doing in the script to the steps outlined earlier in the book.

Model 1:
A Fishbowl Version on *The Pearl,* page 9

Reading of Background and Comprehension Check

Teacher: Okay, so let's stop at the bottom of page 9 and close our books. We're going to do something different, we're going to do a role-play here, which we'll continue in various ways through the rest of the book. We don't want to go any further because we have the conflict but we don't know the resolution yet. We're going to act out those choices. Before we do, let's just make sure we get the situation. Jailene, can you summarize the situation here?

Jailene: Kino and Juana's baby just got bitten by a scorpion and is in danger. They brought him to the doctor.

Teacher: Who else is there?

Derek: There is a crowd of peasants following along.

Teacher: Right. What do we know about the characters?

Derek: Kino, Juana, and the peasants are probably mestizo Mexicans. They are descendants of Europeans and indigenous, or native, Mexicans. They are poorer. Kino doesn't seem to like the doctor because he's of a race that has hurt them. He is probably racist.

Setting the Scene and the Roles

Teacher: We start the scene with the doctor sending his servant out to the door. I'm going to ask a few people to play these roles. Mamadou, you will be Kino. Michelle, you'll be Juana. Elan, you'll be the servant and Andrew will be the doctor. Mamadou (Kino) you have no money to pay the doctor. Okay?

Shania: What do the rest of us do?

Teacher: Five of you will be the peasants who are following along. The rest of you should take one of these scaffolding sheets. You can be a therapist, life coach, or artist. If you're the therapist, for example, you choose one of our characters and really try to get inside his or her head for this scene. Write down what Juana is thinking at various moments. I'm also going to hand a rubric to Julia, Marcos, and Kim. Julia, you'll grade the role-playing of Mamadou. Marcos, you'll do Michelle; Kim, you'll grade Andrew.

Emily: Where do we start?

Identifying the Conflict, the Stakes, and the Choices

Teacher: Those of you in the scene, come to the middle, here. Think about your character. Juana, think about the anguish of having a son who has just been bitten by a scorpion. Doctor, think about how you view these peasants and what you want from them. We are going to start at the moment that Kino and Juana knock on the door and the servant answers. Doctor, you're inside, lounging on a couch. Juana, knock on this table. Before we begin, let's just make sure we know the stakes of this moment. What's at stake here?

Jessica: If Kino and Juana can't get the doctor to treat the baby, he might die. Their family is at stake.

Teacher: And what type of choice do they need to make?

Alberto: They need to figure out how to act with the doctor, how to convince him. They are poor and he's rich. What can they say?

Role-Play of Choice Moment

Teacher: Let's go. 3, 2, 1—action!

Juana knocks on the door.

Servant: What do you want?

Kino: Our baby just got bitten by a scorpion. We need the doctor to treat him.

Servant: Who the heck do you think you are? You need it? Our doctor decides who he treats.

Juana (pleading and rocking a baseball glove as a baby):
Um, please, it is our only son.

Servant: How much money do you have? The doctor is good and he's expensive.

Kino looks at Juana.

Juana: We can't pay him anything now, but we are hard workers, we can work for the money. Please, it is my baby.

Servant: Hold on, let me ask him.

Pausing for Reflection and Advice

Teacher: Okay, let's pause. Let's hear from some of our therapists and life coaches. Charmaine, you are Juana's therapist. What's she thinking?

Charmaine: She's desperate. Her baby's life depends on this moment.

Teacher: And what about our life coaches?

Demi: I'm Juana's coach. I think they need to stay respectful and humble with the doctor.

DJ: I'm Kino's coach and I don't agree. He needs to get assertive and aggressive. He needs to *make* the doctor treat his son.

Reaction of Role-Play

Teacher: Kino and Juana, you need to decide. Let's get back to the scene. 3, 2, 1, and action.

Servant to the Doctor (inside): There are a couple of peasants out there who want you to treat their baby. I guess a scorpion bit him.

Doctor: How much can they pay?

Servant: Nothing. They're poor.

Doctor (laughs): I just treat the ones who can pay me the big bucks. Send them away!

Servant: They seem nice.

Doctor: Send them away!

Servant goes back to Kino and Juana.

Servant: The doctor cannot treat anyone if they don't have the money. I'm sorry. You'll have to try something else.

Juana: Please, please. What can we do? It is my baby.

Kino (starts getting aggressive): This is my son; he's going to die. We need the doctor.

Servant goes to talk to the doctor.

Doctor: If they don't have money, I'm not treating them. There are plenty of clients who will pay. Maybe I'll do it if they agree to become my servants.

Servant (walks back to Juana and Kino): The doctor will treat your son if you agree to be his servant.

Second Pause for Reflection and Advice

Teacher: That was a really great scene. Let's talk about their choice and we'll hear from some of our therapists and photographers to get a sense of what they saw and what they thought was in the heads of the various characters.

Demi: If Kino gets so aggressive, the doctor will never treat him. They need to be respectful.

Mamadou (*Kino*): I tried that. He's not going to help. It won't work. I need to force him to help. I saw a movie with Denzel Washington where a man needed a transplant for his son. He took the hospital hostage. I need to force the doctor.

Michelle (Juana): He's the only doctor. We can't force him.

Teacher: So what are our options? Mamadou and Michelle, I want you to really think about what your character was like in the scene in the book before we role-played and how that will connect to what you do? Let's all find a piece of evidence from the text that clues us about how he'll react.

Students look through text for clues to Kino's temperament and motivations, followed by a brief discussion.

Michelle (Juana): We can't agree to be servants. Who will look after the baby?

Mamadou (Kino): I can be his servant and you look after the baby.

Demi: But then no one will be able to work?

Michelle (Juana): I can become his servant and give Coyotito to my brother to watch.

Teacher: You understand what you're agreeing to?

Michelle (Juana): Yes, but this is my son's life.

Reaction of Role-Play

Teacher: Let's see what happens. 3, 2, 1, Action.

Juana (to the doctor): I will be your servant if you care for our son.

Doctor: No, that's not enough. I want both of you to be servants.

Kino: I need to work to support them. We're poor.

Doctor: That's not my problem.

Kino: She will work for you and I will dive for pearls. The next pearl I find I will give to you.

Doctor: Okay, you have a deal. I will treat your son.

Teacher: Let's see what happens. Remember, this is early twentieth-century medicine. Elizabeth, what number out of 20 do you think the doctor needs to roll to successfully treat a baby from a scorpion bite?

Elizabeth: Maybe a 12?

Teacher: Let's do it.

The doctor rolls; gets a 16.

Debrief: Analysis, Reflections, and Predictions

Teacher: He saves Coyotito. Congratulations Juana and Kino. Now let's talk a bit about their choices and how they feel. Let's think about whether they feel good about themselves and their decisions. And I want to hear from some therapists and life coaches as well as the people who graded their role-play on the rubric.

A discussion ensues.

Teacher: Before we keep reading for homework, let's remember that the author, Steinbeck, now needs to resolve this situation, this conflict, and these choices. Let's make some predictions. Will he write it in the same way that we role-played?

Derek: I know that the baby is going to survive because he's in the picture on the cover.

Mamadou: I don't think he'll treat us well. It will probably go pretty much like our role-play.

Michelle: I don't think he'll treat our son. The author will want to make the best story and it is a better story if he doesn't treat Coyotito and we have to find a way to help him.

Teacher: I like that point that the author will create a great story by increasing the amount of conflict and tension. Let's read the book until the next big choice moment, so we will read for homework until page 20.

Model 2:
A Fishbowl Version on *The Pearl*, page 48

Reading of background and comprehension check

Teacher: We've read up to page 47. The tension is high. Let's stop here so we can role-play the choice moment. What's the situation at this point?

Elizabeth: They're going to sell the pearl.

DJ: The town is thinking about if they would have found it; they're hoping the pearl won't change Kino.

Mamadou: And they're talking about what they'd do if they had the pearl, but I think they're lying when they say they'd share it with the poor.

Identifying the Conflict, the Stakes, and the Choices

Teacher: What's at stake here when they go to sell the pearl?

Gio: Kino and the family could lose respect from everyone else if he makes the wrong decision or gets cheated.

DJ: But what is the right decision?

Elizabeth: The pearl is at stake because it sounds like some of the pearl buyers want to steal it.

DJ: Their child's future is at stake. If someone takes the pearl they're done. All their plans will be finished. If they sell it to a guy for too little, for a mediocre amount, they are barely profiting.

Teacher: How do we know the stakes are high? What are some things that Juana and Kino do that tell us the stakes are high?

Jailene: They get dressed up so they can get more money. They want people to take them seriously.

Kevin: They put the baptism clothes on the baby.

Elizabeth: And all the people in the town are watching them and following them.

Setting the Scene

Teacher: I'm going to ask Kino and Juana to step outside for a moment. *They step outside the room.* Okay, pearl buyers, you need to know that the pearl is worth about 5,000 pesos. Kino and Juana don't know the real value.

DJ: How much is a day's work worth?

Teacher: Let's say about 20 pesos. Now you need to think about your first offer. You two will split the profits, but make it seem like you haven't discussed any of this, like you're not working together.

Role-Playing

Kino and Juana walk back into the room.

Teacher: 3, 2, 1—Action.

Kino: Let me see it.

Juana gives the pearl to Buyer 1.

Kino: How does it look?

Buyer 1 examines it: I think . . . it is good, but it isn't that good.

Juana: It is the biggest pearl you've ever seen.

Kino: It will make your dreams come true.

Buyer 1: I've seen a bunch of things like this in my time.

Pause for Reflection and Advice

Teacher: Let's pause for a second. In Kino and Juana's view how is this playing out so far?

Michelle: I would be kind of angry. Maybe they are offended because they know it is worth more.

Kevin: Kino is getting annoyed because the buyer is trying to make it seem like it isn't worth anything.

Reaction of Role-Play

Teacher: Let's go back in. 3,2,1—action!

Buyer 2: I will give you 300 pesos.

Juana: Noooo.

Kino: That isn't reasonable.

Buyer 2: I'll give you 500 pesos.

Kino: This pearl saved my son's life.

Juana: That isn't enough for my son's future, for him to go to school.

Buyer 2: That isn't my problem.

Second Pause for Reflection and Advice

Teacher: Let's pause. Do we have advice for the sellers or the buyers?
Elizabeth: You should keep going up until they're happy.
Teacher: Do you want to go to another seller?
Demi (Juana): Yes, please!
A third student comes in as the third seller.

Reaction of Role-Play

Teacher: 3, 2, 1—Action!
Juana: If you don't give us a higher amount we'll go to him.
Third Seller: I understand you have a son and I have one too. I understand that. I'm prepared to offer you 700 pesos.
Kino: This pearl healed my son.
Third Seller: That is why I'll give you 800 pesos.
Juana: We will do it for 900 pesos. We want to buy a rifle too and that costs a lot.
Third Seller: You guys are villagers . . . you're coming to sell the pearl and you can go live your little happy life. How long will you last with the pearl unless you sell it? They'll kill him without a rifle. Everyone is coming for you.
Second Seller: Just give me the pearl.

Third Pause for Reflection and Advice

Teacher: Let's pause. Should they take the deal?
Alberto: The money would last them a long time.
Teacher: How were the buyers talking to Kino and Juana?
Elizabeth: They were talking down to them, scaring them.
Zarriah: The sellers need to be more persuasive, not threaten them.

Fourth Pause for Reflection and Advice

Teacher: 3, 2, 1—Action.
Second Seller: 1,500.
Juana: I want to get rid of the pearl.
Kino: We need to think about our life.

Second Seller: 1,800 is my last offer.

Kino and Juana step aside to talk.

Juana: We could die because of this pearl. Someone will kill us because of this pearl. I'll do it for 1,800.

Kino: Think wisely. We need to think of the rest of our son's life.

Third Seller: We can't do 1,800. We were wrong. We will do 1,630 pesos and that is it. We have to make some type of money. We will make only 20 pesos each on this.

Juana: 1,700 pesos. I don't like this.

Second Seller (yelling): 1,630 pesos. That's it.

Third Seller: Think about your son. That's 1,630 reasons why you should take it.

Audience is shouting at Kino and Juana. Juana can't move; she can't make a decision.

Debrief: Analysis, Reflections, and Predictions

Teacher: What is this doing to their marriage?

Kevin: They are having disagreements. It could escalate.

Mamadou: If this doesn't work out they could get killed.

Teacher: Andrew, do you think they were right or wrong to not accept the 1,630 pesos?

Andrew: I think they were right if they want the money to last.

Teacher: How much was it worth?

Zarriah: 5,000 pesos.

Teacher: Now that you know how much it was worth, how does it affect your view of the scene?

Demi: The sellers were liars!

Zarriah: They made the right choice.

Teacher: Even if it were worth 5,000 pesos, does that mean they made the right choice to walk away?

Elizabeth: If they didn't sell the pearl, could they go anywhere else?

Elan: To the capital, but it is a long trip which is money and danger.

Demi: I still think that I'm right. It was a lot of money. I think it is dangerous anyways, so any moment more I have with the pearl it is more danger for us.

Mamadou: People weren't going to like them regardless if they got a lot of money. So he might as well get as much as he can then move away.

Teacher: How do we think Steinbeck will write this scene?

DJ: They will low-ball him.

Mamadou: I think when they low-ball him Kino will get angry but Juana will try to take it.

Elizabeth: I think they won't take it and they'll take the journey to the capital if they can get more money. Bad things will probably happen.

Teacher: What do you mean bad things?

Elizabeth: They could get robbed, get sick. The people in the capital might offer them less.

Michelle: What if Juana walks in and steals the pearl and tries to sell it to the pearl buyers?

Emily: I think Juana will try to steal it to sell it because she is desperate. It is ruining their family. Kino would be furious . . . but I don't really know.

Jailene: I don't think she would steal it; she might want to but I don't think she is capable of doing it; she knows how important the pearl is to Kino. Kino would be really upset. He thinks it holds his future.

Elan: I don't think Juana is that type of person, but if she did Kino would be very upset. He wants to better the whole family.

Model 3:
A Small Group Role-Play on *Fences,* page 66

Teacher: For homework you read up to page 65. What is the last thing Troy says in the reading?

Matthew: He said he needed to tell Rose something.

Teacher: Right, anyone have any predictions about what he might tell her?

Students discuss possible predictions, from losing his job to having an affair.

Teacher: Let's read until the middle of page 66 and I'll stop us when we see the conflict burst out.

Student volunteers read until Troy says "I'm gonna be somebody's daddy."

Teacher: What's the conflict here?

Maria: Wow, Troy is not only having an affair but he's having a baby with another woman.

Teacher: Exactly. This is a real conflict, one that quite a few families actually experience. And here's the choice: Troy, how are you going to explain this to Rose? And Rose, how will you respond? I'm breaking you up in groups of four. One of you will be Rose, one will be Troy, one will be the gamemaster, and one will be an observer (perhaps a therapist). So, we'll have a bunch of different role-plays going on at one time. Gamemasters, you each will have a dice in case you need it. You start the scene and can direct it or throw in new twists if you feel like the characters need it. Pause the scene and call me over if you need help. Therapists, you will share out at the end.

Group 1

Troy: Baby, I'm so sorry, I made a huge mistake. It was a one-time thing. I was with some friends late at night and I met a girl. I didn't even remember her name. She meant nothing to me. I had almost forgotten about her. Rose, you're my girl. You mean everything to me.

Rose (begins to fake cry): How could I mean everything to you and you do that? This is all just talk.

Troy: It isn't talk. You're my wife. I love you. I made a mistake. I'm sorry. I don't know what to do. I messed up.

Rose: What do you want from me? I'm so hurt. I've been with you through everything!

Students pause.

Gamemaster: Rose, what do you want him to do?

Rose: I don't know. I need to think about this . . . Troy, I want you to promise that you'll never see her or the baby ever again.

Group 2

Troy: Rose, listen to me. I'm having a baby with another woman. I've been seeing her for a while. You haven't been the woman I wanted and she gives me what you don't.

Rose: You jerk! How can you say that? Does she cook and clean for you?

Troy: No, but she's there to talk to. And you're always yelling!

Rose (to gamemaster): Can I hit him?

Gamemaster: Yeah, here's the dice. Roll it.

Rose rolls a 6.

Gamemaster: Rose walks up to Troy and smacks him but her fist just bounces off his shoulder. Troy, what do you do?

Troy (thinks a moment): I'm outta here. She's getting violent and I have another woman. I'm just leaving.

Teacher: Okay, all, finish up your scene and therapists need to report back with what happened and what the characters were thinking. I'm really interested in hearing how the various groups responded to this conflict and which responses we think were truest to Wilson's characterization. Then, of course, we'll compare your scenes to what he wrote in *Fences*.

Choice Moments in *The Pearl*[1]

In the chart below (Table 6.1) I outline some of the key choice moments in Steinbeck's *The Pearl*, a classic tale of the fear, greed, and jealousy that can erupt within a family and a community when Kino suddenly strikes it rich by discovering an unusual pearl.

Table 6.1 Suggested Choice Moments for *The Pearl*

Page Number	Characters Involved	The Situation	Choice Moment
9	Kino, Juana, Doctor, Servant	A scorpion has just bitten Kino and Juana's son. They bring him to the office of the wealthy white doctor.	Kino and Juana: How will you approach the doctor? Doctor: What will your response be to Kino and Juana's arrival?
48–9	Kino, Juana, 2 pearl buyers	Kino has gone to the city with Juan Tomas to sell the pearl at the market. Let the sellers know the pearl is worth about 5,000 pesos.	Pearl buyer: How do you respond to Kino and his pearl? Kino: How do you respond to the buyer?
52	Kino, first seller, third seller	The sellers continue to tell Kino the pearl is worthless and they offer 500 pesos, a very low amount.	Kino: What do you do after getting low bids? Sellers: How do you try to convince him?
58	Kino, Juana	Juana decides to steal the pearl in the night. As she leaves, Kino realizes what has happened.	Kino: What do you do? Juana: What do you do?
59	Kino, neighbor	A neighbor sees Kino in the dark and knows that he is alone with the pearl.	Neighbor: What do you do? Kino: What do you do?
60	Kino, Juana	Juana has found that Kino just killed the neighbor.	Juana: How do you respond to the discovery? Kino: How do you respond to Juana?
82	Kino, Juana, 3 trackers	The trackers are near them and two are sleeping by the pool.	Kino and Juana: What do you do with the trackers? What do you do with the pearl?

Choice Moments in *Fences*[2]

Fences depicts a short period in the life of a family that begins to be torn apart as the father (Troy), a reformed criminal, suffers from unaccomplished dreams and family members who do not always follow his lead.

Table 6.2 Suggested Choice Moments for *Fences*

Page Number	Characters Involved	The Situation	Choice Moment
14	Troy, Rose, Lyons	Lyons has arrived to ask his father, Troy, for $10.	Troy: How do you respond to Lyons' request? Lyons and Rose: How do you react to Troy?
35	Troy, Cory	Troy wants Cory to work at the A&P but Cory wants to play football for the team. Cory has the chance for college recruitment.	Cory: What request do you make to Troy? Troy: How do you respond to Cory?
57	Troy, Cory, Rose	Troy has told the coach that Cory can no longer play because he lied about working at A&P.	Cory: What do you say to your father? Rose and Troy: How do you respond to Cory?
66	Troy, Rose	Troy has begun to tell Rose that he is going to have a baby with another woman.	Troy: How do you explain this to Rose? Rose: What is your response?
72	Troy, Rose, Cory	Cory has arrived just as Troy has grabbed Rose's arm violently during an argument.	Cory: What do you do when you see this? Rose and Troy: How do you respond?
78	Troy, Rose	Troy has arrived with his new baby and asks Rose to care for the baby.	Troy: How do you make the request? Rose: How do you react?
85	Troy, Cory	Troy and Cory get in an argument as Cory tries to walk by. Troy insists that he say "excuse me."	Cory: What do you do? Troy: What is your response?

Choice Moments in *Of Mice and Men*[3]

Of Mice and Men is the classic depression-era tale of the complicated friendship between George and Lenny, and the ways in which internal and external conflicts can get in the way of our dreams. The book builds the characters considerably for the first 50 or so pages until we reach the choice moments.

Table 6.3 Suggested Choice Moments for *Of Mice and Men*

Page Number	Characters Involved	The Situation	Choice Moment
62	Curley, George, Lenny	Curley is angry and looking for a fight. He notices Lenny laughing and says "What the hell you laughin' at?"	Lenny: How do you respond? Curley and George: How do you react to the situation?
77–80	Lenny, Candy, Crooks	Candy arrives and is lonely and clearly looking for attention. Crooks understands the danger of speaking with Curley's wife.	Candy: What do you want from Crooks and Lenny? Crooks and Lenny: How do you respond to Candy?
91	Candy, Lenny	Lenny has been stroking Candy's hair and unwittingly has done it too powerfully. She begins to protest.	Candy: What do you do and say? Lenny: How do you respond?
92	Lenny	Lenny realizes that he has accidentally killed Candy	Lenny: What do you do?
104–5	George, Lenny	The search party is out to find Lenny. They are closing in but Lenny has found George first.	Lenny: What do you want from George? George: What do you say to Lenny? What do you do to him?

Choice Moments in *Death of a Salesman*[4]

Death of a Salesman tells the story of Willy, a late middle-aged salesman whose job, dreams, and family all visibly unravel as it becomes clear that the near fantasy world that he has built up around his image and his sons is all an illusion.

Table 6.4 Suggested Choice Moments for *Death of a Salesman*

Page Number	Characters Involved	The Situation	Choice Moment
60	Willy, Howard	Willy understands that he can no longer function as a traveling salesman and needs a job in New York. He goes to ask Howard, his boss, for a transfer and a fixed salary.	Willy: How do you approach Howard? What do you ask for and how do you ask it? Howard: How do you respond to Willy?
75	Willy, Charley	Willy asks his cousin Charley for money. Instead, Charley offers him a job.	Willy: How do you respond to Charley's offer? Charley: How do you react to Willy?
83–4	Willy, Biff, Happy	Father and sons are having dinner to celebrate their success. However, Willy has been fired and Biff wants to tell his father that he was not able to get hired by Oliver.	Biff: What do you tell Willy? How? Willy: What do you tell Biff? How do you respond to each other?
93	Willy, Biff, Woman	Biff has gone to visit Willy on the road, arrives at his hotel room, and hears a woman's voice in the bathroom.	Biff: What do you do when you hear the woman's voice? Willy: How do you respond to Biff?

Choice Moments in *A Raisin in the Sun*[5]

A Raisin in the Sun depicts the multi-generational Younger family as they attempt to improve their fortunes by capitalizing on the insurance money left by Mama's husband and Walter's father.

Table 6.5 Suggested Choice Moments for *A Raisin in the Sun*

Page Number	Characters Involved	The Situation	Choice Moment
38	Walter, Ruth, Beneatha	Walter and Beneatha begin to discuss their father's insurance money. Walter wants it to start a liquor business but Beneatha wants it for medical school.	Walter: How do you convince Beneatha and Ruth? Beneatha: How do you convince Walter and Ruth?
51	Mama, Ruth, Beneatha	Mama and Beneatha are in an argument and Beneatha says she does not believe in God. Mama is religious.	Mama: How do you respond to Beneatha's declaration? Beneatha: How do you respond to Mama?
70	Walter, Mama, Ruth	The check has arrived. Ruth is pregnant but has not told Walter.	Walter: What do you do and say when the check arrives? Ruth: What do you tell Walter?
75	Walter, Mama, Ruth	Mama has just told Walter that Ruth is pregnant and thinking of an abortion.	Walter: What do you say? Ruth: How do you respond?
90–2	Walter, Mama, Ruth, Travis, Beneatha	Mama has just spent the money and will tell the family how.	Mama: Decide how you will spend the money and then tell the family. Walter, Ruth, Beneatha: How do you respond?
118	Lindner, Walter, Beneatha, Ruth	Lindner has arrived from their new neighborhood's welcoming committee to try to discourage them from moving to a white neighborhood.	Lindner: What do you tell the family? How do you try to discourage them? Walter, Ruth, Beneatha: How do you respond?

continued

Table 6.5 continued

Page Number	Characters Involved	The Situation	Choice Moment
129	Walter, Beneatha, Mama	Walter has lost all of the money. He did not deposit the money for Beneatha's education and instead spent it on his liquor store and it was stolen.	Walter: What do you tell them? How? Beneatha, Mama: How do you respond?
147	Lindner, Walter, Beneatha, Ruth	After having lost their money, the family calls Mr. Lindner back.	Walter: What do you say to Mr. Lindner? Mr. Lindner: How do you respond?

Notes

1 Steinbeck, J. (1992). *The Pearl*. New York: Penguin Books.
2 Wilson, A. (1986). *Fences*. New York: Plume.
3 Steinbeck, J. (1993). *Of Mice and Men*. New York: Penguin Books.
4 Miller, A. (1998). *Death of a Salesman*. New York: Penguin Books.
5 Hansberry, L. (1994). *A Raisin in the Sun*. New York: Vintage Books.

Conclusion

Once you have immersed yourself and your students in role-plays the opportunities begin to seem limitless. My experience with this strategy started with historical role-plays but as this book demonstrates, recent forays into literature role-plays have shown that the spectrum of possibilities there are just as vast, if not more so, and the outcomes just as rich. If literature is partly about understanding what it means to be human, then role-plays work not simply to help students understand characters but also to have a deeper sense of humanity.

Even within other fields of social studies, role-plays function to illuminate difficult ideas and to bring dryer topics to life. Many teachers have told me that some of their best lessons are economic simulations that immerse students in the industrial revolution, factories, a capitalist system or a communist system. This does not surprise me. When topics are more difficult or more arcane, innovative teachers come up with their best work – and many times that results in simulations or role-plays. These may be single lesson experiences rather than fully fleshed-out units but they serve a crucial purpose. We all, in fact, largely understand free-market economics simply by living in a capitalist economy. Economic role-plays provide that experience for students alongside graphs and equations. A number of excellent economic simulations are available online.

One of my earliest role-plays, in fact, falls into this category. I was teaching a basic global history survey course and trying to figure out what to do with the Silk Road and the central concept of "cultural diffusion." I began to ponder the idea of recreating a Silk Road market in the classroom. I did some research on the types of products sold along the trade route and put together biographies for about fifteen archetypal characters ranging from Iraqi date sellers to Chinese paper merchants. Each biography included something for the character to sell, three products to buy (and the reason why), and the ideal buying/selling prices. The prices I gave for the buyers were always lower than for the sellers. For example, the Iraqi date seller wanted to sell his product for $5 but the Sogdian wine merchant's biography urged him to purchase it for $2. This arrangement compelled all students to negotiate. I made a stop at Canal Street in Chinatown to purchase cheap imitation silk, herbal medicines, and fake swords. A few students helped me hand-make some of the other products. Lastly, their instructions required them to "culturally diffuse" some aspect of their culture or religion (found in their brief biographies) to another character during each purchase or sale. The day of the Silk Road market was always a hit.

Teachers often wonder what their practice will look like five, ten, or twenty years down the road. I, certainly, am in a far different place than I was when I began. For me, one of the most important elements in my work is to remain engaged and excited about what I do. To some extent, that can come through changing the content I teach, taking on school leadership opportunities, or writing. More than anything, though, I find it is the anticipation each semester for the role-play unit that keeps my juices flowing. I may tire a bit of teaching reading annotation or paragraph structure but I never grow weary of role-play. In fact, I often find myself in the faculty room afterwards bubbling (and babbling) enthusiastically and somewhat embarrassingly about the students' choices that day, even in a scenario I've done time and time again. But there are worse things than that, I'm sure. And I hope this practice brings you the same excitement year after year as it does for me – because the real winners, then, will be the students.